CONTENTS

PART THREE
CRITICAL APPROACHES

PART FOUR
CRITICAL PERSPECTIVES

PART FIVE
BACKGROUND

PART ONE

INTRODUCTION

STUDYING POEMS

Reading poems and exploring them critically can be approached in a number of ways, but when reading a poem for the first time it is a good idea to consider some, or all, of the following:

- **Format and style:** how do poems differ from other **genres** of text? Does the poem capture a single moment in time, tell a whole story, or make a specific point?

- **The poet's perspective:** consider what the poet has to say, how he or she presents a particular view of people, the world, society, ideas, issues, etc. Are, or were, these views controversial?

- **Verse and metre:** how are **stanzas** or patterns of lines used to reveal the **narrative**? What rhythms and rhymes does the poet use to convey an atmosphere or achieve an effect?

- **Choice of language:** does the poet choose to write formally or informally? Does he or she use different registers for different voices in the poem, vary the sound and style, employ literary techniques such as **imagery**, **alliteration** and **metaphor**?

- **Links and connections:** what other texts does this poem remind you of? Can you see connections between its narrative, main characters and ideas and those of other texts you have studied? Is the poem part of a literary movement or tradition?

- **Your perspective and that of others:** what are your feelings about the poem? Can you relate to its emotions, **themes** and ideas? What do others say about the poem – for example critics or other poets and writers?

These York Notes offer an introduction to John Clare's poetry and cannot substitute for close reading of the text and the study of secondary sources.

> **CONTEXT**
>
> The word 'poetry' comes from the Greek word *poesis*, meaning 'making' or 'creating'. People have been writing poetry for thousands of years – the earliest we have dates back to c.3000 BC.

READING JOHN CLARE'S POETRY

John Clare (1793–1864) is best known for his important voice as a peasant poet, and as a **dialect** poet. For many critics, he is the most accomplished of the peasant poets, and the circumstances of his poverty, mental illness and incarceration feed into his poems a great deal of poignancy and emotional interest. He is also – and for some, more importantly – a poet of the natural world. His work concentrates on describing the natural world in extraordinary detail. For others, he is a political poet. He laments the enclosing of common land on which the poor had been free to let their animals graze, and the wanderer had been free to roam.

Much of Clare's writing is focused on crossing boundaries of various kinds. 'Sonnet: "I dreaded walking where there was no path"' looks at the fear felt by someone who is trespassing, and recalls a similar scene in William Wordsworth's *The Prelude* (published posthumously in 1850), where as a boy Wordsworth borrowed a boat without permission and rode out onto the lake. In his **sonnet** Clare writes that he 'fancied every stranger frowned at me' (8), and in Wordsworth's poem too, guilt is a tangible presence. Contrastingly, in 'Emmonsales Heath' Clare explores the wonder and importance of open land that is 'Untouched' (26) by man.

Clare's poetry emerged at a time when there was an increasing interest in writing that was local to a particular setting (**loco-descriptive**). Clare is very particular about describing local customs and agricultural practices in his poetry. He worked as an agricultural labourer until he was incarcerated in a lunatic asylum, and he took great pleasure in recording, remembering and taking part in local customs of various kinds. In 'December' from *The Shepherd's Calendar*: 'Christmas' he writes: 'Old customs, O I love the sound, / However simple they may be' (41). Part of the purpose of poetry for Clare is to record this dying culture: the 'merry crew / Bedecked in masks and ribbons gay / The "Morris dance"' (65–7). Yet, in writing about the rural poor, Clare is largely unsentimental, preferring **realism**. 'The foddering boy' (1), for instance, in the poem of that name, is merely described as cold. Clare avoids sentiment by concentrating on the tasks that the boy is performing.

His 'Song: "She tied up her few things"' is closer to sentiment, however, describing a poor itinerant worker packing up her things and leaving to go home.

Much of Clare's life was financially difficult, as he lived through the agricultural depression of the first few decades after the end of the Napoleonic Wars in 1815. The cost of labour slumped to almost the level of parish relief (a charitable donation that could take the form of money or housing), and we know of occasions when Clare was starving for want of food. His education was meagre, and, though he read as much as he could, books were expensive. That he wrote at all is a remarkable accomplishment; that he wrote sensitive poems which explore a range of emotional and natural experiences is astounding. In spite of his poor education, Clare had a keen ear for popular discourse. His writing includes work that is classed as **picturesque**, a literary way of writing about nature in the eighteenth century and early nineteenth century.

Clare's life as a poet transported him into a literary world that was both exciting and terrifying. One of his main **themes** deals with how he understood the fame that his poetry brought him. His poems reveal that he feared his loss of privacy, and longed for solitude and the comfort of home. He also felt like an outsider. Much of his work explores the emotions of being a solitary person in a community, or being on the margins of a community. Spanning emotional complexity, such as that seen in 'I Am' and 'Love and Memory', and simple realism, such as 'Sonnet: "The maiden ran away"', the poems reveal an immense talent for description. Not all are serious, however. 'The Parish', for example, is a carefully observed **satire** on social climbing. In this poem, the genuine woman, 'red and rosy as the lovely spring' (146), is more beautiful than the woman who apes the accomplishments of her social superiors; and, importantly, she has a stronger relationship with the outdoors.

Literary tradition also exercises Clare to a considerable degree. He argues that nature should be observed directly, and that a poet should not merely repeat what tradition has already associated with a particular bird or animal. The nightingale, for instance, is for Clare in 'The Nightingale's Nest' a happy bird, and not the **melancholy** bird

CONTEXT

In the Poor Law Act of 1601 Elizabeth I made the poor the responsibility of the local parish, and ensured that landowners and tenants paid a tax that went to the local poor when they were ill or unemployed. There were often degrading conditions attached to receiving parish relief, such as entering the workhouse. The Poor Law was amended in 1834, making it more difficult to avoid the workhouse. Workhouses, famously described in Charles Dickens's *Oliver Twist* (1837–8), were little more than prisons.

CONTEXT

Cowper, known for his progressive views on slavery, animal rights and equality, was an important early influence on the Romantic movement. His conversational style influenced the work of William Wordsworth (1770–1850) and Samuel Taylor Coleridge (1772–1834).

 CHECK THE BOOK

John Goodridge and Kelsey Thornton note that Clare's trespassing is prompted by his guilt at 'stealing time from his employer' ('John Clare: the trespasser' in *John Clare in Context*, edited by Hugh Haughton, Adam Phillips and Geoffrey Summerfield, 1994, p. 90): 'Having stolen his employer's time, and obtained a precious piece of the culture which all his training has taught him is not for the likes of him, he must guiltily hide his crime.'

of literary tradition. That is not to say that literary tradition meant nothing to Clare; his favourite poets, such as William Cowper (1731–1800), James Thomson (1700–48), William Collins (1721–59) and Thomas Gray (1716–71), were important to him. The work of Cowper, in particular, inspired Clare's **conversation poems**.

Most of Clare's poetry is **lyrical** and written from the perspective of a single speaker, though not necessarily from the perspective of the poet himself. In reading any poem it is important to acknowledge that multiple interpretations can be made, whether one imagines Clare himself as the speaker, or that he is speaking through a **persona**. Given that Clare's poetry is intertwined with the experiences and events of his own life, there are grounds for assuming that, in most cases, he is the speaker. Nevertheless, in reading any poem, one should be cautious about these assumptions; poets may draw on the events of their own lives, but also build on these and include emotions they have never experienced and events that never happened. In most cases in these Notes, the speaker is referred to as 'the poet'; with those poems that have an explicitly autobiographical inflection, it seems reasonable to assume that the authorial voice is Clare's own. He, for example, trespassed onto an estate and felt guilty about it, just as we see in 'Sonnet: "I dreaded walking where there was no path"'.

John Clare's poetry is rich with the life and customs of the nineteenth century. We gain from him a view of the simple country life, imagined not from the perspective of the sophisticated bourgeois educated man, but from the perspective of a man who lived this life and endured its hardships. Clare is also an important voice for those who have experienced disability. As the work of a sufferer of mental illness who was confined to an institution, Clare's poetry reveals the anxieties of a man unsure of his identity, and for whom the curtailments of institutionalisation and separation from the world he knew and loved were painful. Furthermore, his work reveals much about the nature of editorial practices of the nineteenth century. In studying Clare's poetry we gain insight into the workings of the mind of a unique man, whose ambition to become a famous poet marked him out as separate from his community, but also the voice of his community.

PART TWO

THE TEXT

NOTE ON THE TEXT

The edition of John Clare's poetry used in the preparation of these Notes is the 1997 Everyman's Poetry edition, edited by R. K. R. Thornton. Most of the poems included here were either published after Clare had died or were published in newspapers and annuals. Four collections of poetry were published during Clare's lifetime: *Poems Descriptive of Rural Life and Scenery. By John Clare, A Northamptonshire Peasant* (1820), *The Village Minstrel and Other Poems* (1821), *The Shepherd's Calendar, with Village Stories and Other Poems* (1827) and *The Rural Muse* (1835). This is, however, only a fraction of the writing that he produced. Clare's manuscripts were recently edited for Oxford University Press by Eric Robinson, David Powell and P. M. S. Dawson. Many of the poems of the Everyman anthology belong to *The Midsummer Cushion*. This was a collection that existed only in manuscript form until 1979. The Northborough **sonnets** were written between 1832 and 1837 and, with the exception of those that were included in *The Rural Muse* or in newspapers, these were not published until 1995. The Everyman anthology lists poems thematically rather than in chronological order.

DETAILED SUMMARIES

A COUNTRY VILLAGE YEAR

SONNET: 'I DREADED WALKING WHERE THERE WAS NO PATH'

- Clare recalls trespassing and the feelings of guilt that accompanied the experience.
- He concludes that he is glad he has never owned a country estate, as this would make him feel lonely.

CONTEXT

Eric Robinson, David Powell and P. M. S. Dawson note that the poem may be taken as a condensed version of Clare's early poem 'Narrative verses Written after an Excursion from Helpston to Burghley Park'. Burghley House, home of the earl of Exeter, was about four and a half miles from Helpston. Clare was an apprentice kitchen gardener there in 1807.

CHECK THE BOOK

The laws against trespass and poaching were harsh. John Goodridge and Kelsey Thornton observe that if 'the gamekeeper who accused him of poaching' had been believed, 'Clare could have been sentenced to imprisonment, with the possibility of a public whipping and/or hard labour, or (after 1816) seven years' transportation' ('John Clare: the trespasser' in *John Clare in Context*, edited by Hugh Haughton, Adam Phillips and Geoffrey Summerfield, 1994, p. 98).

Clare remembers a beautiful day when he walked across land that belonged to someone else. Even though he was scared of being caught, he experienced the beauty of the landscape, and so continued to trespass. Later, having reached the road, Clare imagined that everyone he passed was aware of his guilt. Since then, he has often thought of this particular day and concluded that it would be wonderful to own such a place. The poet's consolation is that as he owns no land, he never feels alone, as landownership isolates people from their community.

COMMENTARY

This poem links with one of Clare's central **themes**: the politics of rights of way. Clare thought that the countryside should be for everyone. As discussed in **Reading John Clare's poetry**, much of Clare's verse is about different kinds of boundaries: the boundaries of the lunatic asylum he was imprisoned in, the isolation of solitary characters, the way in which animals and plants are free from the restriction of boundaries, and the breaking down of boundaries within communities. His poetry also expresses the joy of wandering unrestricted, as if without boundaries. In this poem Clare has clearly used someone else's property as his own, and this causes him anxiety. The **syntax** – repeating 'And' at the start of lines 2, 3, 4, 7, 9 and 14 – heightens the tension. If one is recounting something in a breathless way, one is careless about how one links sentences; the 'and' repetition echoes this by forcing the reader to carry on without a break. The poem ends with a maxim-like **couplet** in which Clare sums up his creed: he is never alone because he owns nothing, and he cannot use other people's property as his own. Perhaps we are meant to conclude that he has learned from the experience of trespassing that he must not take what does not belong to him. There is, nevertheless, such a strong feeling of appreciation of the beauty of the land on which he trespasses that the creed is somewhat undermined. The penultimate line of the **sonnet**, 'But having nought I never feel alone' (13), is puzzling. Presumably the idea is that by having no land, Clare does not experience the isolation of owning a country estate. The poem shows that the land on which Clare is free to walk is land on which he can share experiences with other people. He is, therefore, never alone.

GLOSSARY

2   **swath** row of scythed hay left to dry

SONNET: 'THE PASSING TRAVELLER'

- A pit of trees provides an unusual split-level landscape.
- The pit is so deep that it appears as though it could contain a whole church.

Clare comments that an 'ancient stone pit full of trees' (2) is a remarkable sight for a passing traveller because it is extremely deep. When viewed from above, the scene gives a topsy-turvy perspective.

COMMENTARY

In contrast with many of Clare's poems, which stress the familiarity of landscapes, this poem centres on the experience of those who are surprised by the unfamiliarity of a landscape. The passing traveller marvels at a sight that is new to him, and the boy, who is broadening his experience of his locality, also encounters the unexpected. It is no surprise to the reader, then, that the **discourse** of the **sublime** is invoked. The sublime aesthetic stresses the extremes of landscape, focusing on the experience as awe-inspiring. Several Romantic poets use this kind of language. Percy Bysshe Shelley (1792–1822), for instance, chooses the Swiss Alps as his sublime subject in 'Mont Blanc' (1816). In Clare's poem, the 'passing stranger' often stops at the scene and looks with 'wonder' (5) because it is so unusual, and thinks that he could walk on the treetops. His perspective, looking down on the crow and its nest, is godlike and unnatural; while the boy, who is in the pit killing bees, takes a risk by climbing up the highest tree to find a magpie's nest, and is also amazed to discover he has only reached ground level. While small details of nature are described here – the 'black-nosed bee' (11) and crow's eggs – the overriding sense is of wonder and awe, in keeping with the theme of the sublime.

CONTEXT

Both 'Sonnet: "I dreaded walking where there was no path"' and 'Sonnet: "The passing traveller"' belong to the Northborough sonnets (see **Note on the text**). The former sonnet is unusual in that it uses **rhyming couplets**. These may add to the theme of never being alone, as the paired lines accompany each other.

 CHECK THE POEM

In 'Mont Blanc' Shelley describes his awe at seeing a 'dark, deep Ravine' (12). He calls it an 'awful scene' (15), meaning that it is awe-inspiring. The repetition of 'deep' in Clare's poem also recalls he 'Lines Composed a Few Miles above Tintern Abbey' (1798), in which Wordsworth refers to the 'steep and lofty cliffs' of a 'wild secluded scene' that impress 'Thoughts of more deep seclusion' on his mind (5–7).

CONTEXT

Emmonsales Heath, sometimes known as Helpston Heath or Ailsworth Heath, is grazing land south of Helpston, Clare's home village. The poem is part of *The Midsummer Cushion* collection of poems and dates to February 1823.

CHECK THE POEM

Clare also wrote a **sonnet** called 'Emmonsales Heath in Winter', which focuses mainly on the poet's love for the birds of the heath.

EMMONSALES HEATH

- Clare contemplates the ancient heath, describing its flora and fauna.
- Nature seems to protect its family on the heath, and offers places of beauty and seclusion.
- As a child, the poet often walked on the heath in spring, feeling joyful, close to nature and to God.

Clare finds that the heath still looks ancient because it has never been ploughed. Since it is untouched, the land has a wildness to it that makes it special and, to some extent, sacred. It is impossible to wander over land such as this and not leave one's cares behind. Clare suggests that anyone who does not feel the peace in such places has no love, does not understand poetry, and cannot see the benefit of solitude. When the poet was a boy, he walked across this heath on May Day. This experience made him happy, and he felt that God was being kind to him to fill him with such joy.

COMMENTARY

The poem does not tell a story, but muses on a number of natural scenes connected with the heath. The poet addresses the heath using a mixture of formal language ('thy' and 'thee') and ordinary speech. Emmonsales Heath is **personified**, and is described as being dressed in 'wild garb' (1), suggesting that its clothes are natural and it has not been touched by humanity. The heath is 'lingering' (2), because it has not yet been swept away by modern changes. Like the moor in 'The Moors' it has an 'eternal' quality ('The Moors', 2). The naturalness of the landscape is contrasted with the unnaturalness of farming. Farming – 'industry' (9) – is associated with pride, and a never-ending need to continue to destroy the natural landscape. The heath, nevertheless, has been spared, and its purity is compared to that of a 'maiden' (11) or virgin. Farming is here sexualised, and sexuality is assumed to be negative.

The scene moves to the wildlife associated with the heath, and here we can see the beginnings of the interference of people. Clare opens with the reassuring image of birds building their nests in spring, but continues with the image of the hare being hunted by 'savage men' (16). Swains (shepherds or farm labourers) and maidens, however, are integrated harmoniously into the landscape. The swains rest, and the maidens gather wild flowers. Nature, personified, protects its family (of animals and plants) using the security provided by the heath. Its remoteness from interference means that flowers can find 'peaceful homes' (20) there. Clare repeats the same sentiments in a religious context, suggesting that the heath has continued untouched since Eden. The intermingling grass is the same as it has always been; the soothing brook has retained its freedom to thread (like cotton) lawlessly wherever it wants to go.

No one can pass such beauty without wanting to stay and look at it. Clare observes that he has often come across wild places like this and did not fail to share in their sweetness, and blessed them. To him, a person who can feel the wind blowing across such places without wanting to live there has a heart that is 'dead to quiet hours' (53) – incapable of relaxing – is unable to love, does not experience the benefits of solitude, and cannot read poetry. Poetry is here characterised as a flowering plant, a particularly fitting **metaphor** for nature poetry. Clare returns again to the description of important natural places, using elevated language and the vocative case ('O') to express this (41 and 57). Spring, like nature also personified, loves to begin the flowering early here because it is protected from 'Winter's wind' (60). The spring flowers, cowslips, surprise the children because they come before April.

The poet then recalls his own childhood, and the walks he took on the heath on May Day (the first of May). May Day indicates the beginning of summer, hence the dry paths, leaves on the trees and ankle-deep grass. At this time, he says, he remembers thinking for hours in the sun, and thinking about the things his childhood friends had said when playing. These children are characterised as imaginative: 'fancy tries its wings' (72). Clare's depiction of childhood is similar to that seen in Wordsworth's poetry. It is a time

CONTEXT

May Day features in Wordsworth's *The Prelude* (finished in 1805, revised by Wordsworth for much of his life and published posthumously in 1850) and in William Blake's *Songs of Innocence and of Experience* (1794). The festival usually involved setting up a maypole and dancing around it, or parading with dolls or collections of silver. Romantic writers became interested in the festival when its practice began to decline, using it to express their close connections to local traditions, and to celebrate the beauties of nature. See *The Romantics and the May Day Tradition* by Essaka Joshua (2007).

QUESTION

How does what Clare has to say about the state of the countryside in 'Emmonsales Heath' compare with what he says in 'The Moors'?

of joy, imaginative freedom and closeness to nature: 'all life's little crowd' (74) – the whole of the natural world – sang because it was happy. This closeness is evidence of the kindness of God, 'that mighty power' (77), who, like a sun, spread his beams across the poet's childhood. The association of the sun with God is a classical tradition (Apollo, the sun god, was also the god of poetry), but it is also a Christian tradition (Psalm 84:11 states: 'For the Lord God is a sun and shield'). The poet observes that God filled everyone with joy, regardless of class, and even the ants seemed as blessed as he. Here he implies that God shines on both the small and the great. The sun, at the end of the poem, becomes a **symbol** of hope; it is seen plainly by everyone; its halo (suggesting its religious importance) is the light that emanates from it; and it cheers everyone. Importantly, the sky is 'common' (87); it, like God, is for everyone and 'every thing' (88). In a similar way, the poem 'Shadows of Taste' ends with an image of the sun, **symbolising** wisdom, beaming its rays.

GLOSSARY		
1	**garb**	clothing
3	**Furze**	gorse, a spiny evergreen shrub
7	**blythe**	happy
8	**ploughshares**	large pointed blades of a plough
22	**woodbines**	climbing plants, especially honeysuckle
23	**sojourning**	staying in a place temporarily
29	**ling**	heather
	brake	large ferns, especially bracken
37	**rude**	wild
55	**Poesy**	poetry
64	**rime**	frost
83	**pismires**	ants

THE SUMMER SHOWER

- The poet observes a summer shower from a hidden spot in the countryside.
- The rain becomes heavier and people run for shelter.
- A woman slips over in the mud on her way home, while some boys searching for nests are trapped by an aggressive bull.
- The summer shower brings joy to the people and animals.

Clare describes his appreciation of a refreshing summer rain shower, while sitting in a secluded place. A group of people weeding the cornfields dash for cover and exchange stories. On her way home a beautiful woman slips in the mud, and is teased by a farmhand. Boys who are stealing birds' eggs wait impatiently for the rain to pass. The plough horse and the farmhands enjoy the release the shower brings.

COMMENTARY

This poem concentrates in detail on the responses of people, animals and plants to the rain. Clare declares that he profoundly loves 'to spend a quiet hour' (2) hidden away in the woods, listening to the summer shower. His description of the woods as 'crowding' (2) suggests that the forest is dense, but also that he is, in some sense, not alone. The rain is soothing like 'balm' (5), its coolness is refreshing in the heat of the day, and he can feel it on his hands, which he holds in the air almost as if in prayer. Clare's connection with things outside of the self sets the **tone** for the poem, which is a list of scenes linked together with conjunctives such as 'and'. He plays with the idea of being a poet hidden in a canopy of leaves, but he is also a **narrator** who describes more than he can possibly see from this vantage point. He is exploring, then, his fictional perspective as well as his real perspective.

CONTEXT

This poem is part of *The Midsummer Cushion* collection and was composed between 1819 and 1832. It is written in the **ballad stanza** (with the rhyme scheme *abab*), a simple and traditional form for peasant poetry. *The Midsummer Cushion* was the title chosen by Clare for what was to be his last volume of poetry published during his lifetime, and he originally chose over 350 poems for this collection. But Clare's patron, Eliza Emmerson, particularly liked 'The Rural Muse', which was intended to be the first poem in *The Midsummer Cushion*, and so eventually the collection, much reduced, was published under the title *The Rural Muse* in 1835.

CHECK THE POEM

Clare's enclosure in his leafy bower, separate from the people he observes, links him to the gypsies in the poem. Here the gypsies pay no attention to the showers, in their 'blanket camps' (81; this possibly means tents), as they are sheltered by blackthorn bushes. Clare frequently refers to gypsies in his poems as outsiders – see 'The Gipsy Camp' and 'Sonnets: The Hedgehog'.

QUESTION

Look at some other seasonal poems by Clare, 'Summer Tints', 'Winter Fields' and 'Sonnet: "The landscape laughs in Spring"'. What different types of language does Clare use to describe these contrasting times of year?

Clare's impression of the summer shower is that it connects a range of people and animals through collective experience. He describes in close detail the happiness of the woodchat and the blackbird sitting on her nest, safely hidden in ivy in a remote part of the forest. Meanwhile the pettichap is searching for food, like a mouse, and is quite close to where the poet is. Her nest is like an 'oven house' (19) and, even though it is at ground level, it is safely hidden away from those who collect eggs. The poet thus distinguishes himself from the spoiler of nature – 'the pilfering boy' (24) – who does not know that the nest is there. The poet is special in that he is both a knowledgeable and a benign presence in the natural world. Clare had a fascination for nests, mentioning them in many of his poems; 'The Nightingale's Nest' and 'The Yellowhammer's Nest' are two that focus on the topic.

Although disruption is at the heart of the events concerning the human workers in the poem – the rain interferes with activities of the 'weeding troop' (33) – there is no disruption to the sense of community. The group rush for cover under some old willow trees and sing **ballads** while they wait for it to stop. They share endless and far-fetched stories, until the rain looks like it is going to get heavier and they decide that it is preferable to return home. The noise of the showers is likened to humming, suggesting that nature has a harmonious music of its own. The weeders enjoy the rain, jumping over the brook that 'mutters through the weeds' (42) as if rushing off to find a quieter place where it can greet the rain – now **personified** as a pretty person with dimples – giving us the impression that the 'hasty brook' (41) is a lover who is in search of his mistress. A beautiful woman (or perhaps Beauty personified) slips over in the mud, and blushes because her ankle has been revealed, something that would have been thought immodest at the time. She is secretly pleased that it has been seen, though, because she knows that it is beautiful. Behind her is a rough peasant, who makes 'vulgar gibes' (54), probably of a sexual nature, and the woman is momentarily afraid of climbing over the stile in front of him. She teases the man in order to make sure that he behaves himself, and thus the moment of disharmony is quickly dispelled by humour.

Leisure is also an important aspect of the poem. A boy sits lazily on the horse as the plough team 'wet and dripping plashes' (73) heads home in the rain ('plash' is an **onomatopoeic** word meaning 'splash'), which makes a loud and happy song. The horse is then released from the plough, and chews the wet grass beneath the leafy archway of dripping branches 'loaded' with water (78). The fieldworkers are wet but happy, and sing a 'loud and merry song' (76). The emotional landscape of the poem is concerned with joy and calm; calmness, personified, 'Breathes a refreshing sense of strengthening power' (90). This kind of calm and strength is likened to that felt by those who work hard and have Sunday off: 'toil' (91) is also personified as part of this **allusion**.

The poem ends with a description of the 'cramped horizon' (105) – possibly an allusion to the sun going down. Clare personifies the evening, in this final **stanza**, in the manner of William Collins's poem 'Ode to Evening', where evening brings joy: 'Summer loves to sport / Beneath thy ling'ring light' (43–4). The poems have a number of things in common: both poets describe nature in detail and discuss its musicality, and the speakers of both poems experience the landscape from a hidden place. Clare knew Collins's work from a young age, and, as Mark Storey observes in *The Poetry of John Clare: A Critical Introduction* (1974), was reading Collins's work at the time he was writing 'The Summer Shower' and may have been drawn to this poet by an extreme episode of depression. Collins is noted for his descriptions of **melancholy** (another term for depression). Clare included 'Ode to Evening' in his list of favourite poems, and observed that Collins was a poet who 'went to nature' for his images.

CONTEXT

Collins is famous for his **odes**, the most famous of which is 'Ode to Evening' (1746). He was a close observer of the natural world, greatly admired by the Romantic poets, and his work was heavily influenced by classical literature.

 CHECK THE BOOK

Storey notes that Clare experimented with the stanza form that Collins used for 'Ode to Evening' in the period in which he was writing 'The Summer Shower' (*The Poetry of John Clare: A Critical Introduction*, 1974, p. 129).

GLOSSARY		
1	**o'ercanopied**	covered over
4	**list**	listen to
12	**woodchat**	garden warbler
17	**Pettichap**	willow warbler
18	**nimbling**	darting
	arbour	shady retreat
19	**oven house**	village bakery

continued

CHECK THE BOOK

You can read some of Collins's **odes**, including 'Ode to Evening', in *The New Oxford Book of Eighteenth-Century Verse*, chosen and edited by Roger Lonsdale (1984).

21	**wood-bents** bent wood
29	**meeds** meadows
45	**drabble** trail in the mud
46	**elting** damp, recently ploughed
58	**assails** makes a verbal attack on
61	**Birdnesting** searching for birds' nests
80	**Naps** bites
82	**blackthorns** also called sloes
94	**dells** small valleys

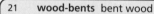

SONNET: 'THE MAIDEN RAN AWAY'

- A maiden dashes to fetch her washing and is wet through to the skin.
- People and birds are almost drowned by the downpour.

The poem describes the sudden effect of torrential rain on the animals and people of the countryside. Women scream with distress when the water floods their homes; work stops; and a very deep stone pit fills to the top with water.

COMMENTARY

CHECK THE POEM

Anna Barbauld's poem 'Washing-Day' (1797) explores with humour the ordinariness of a washing day. Among other things, the poem describes how intrusive washing is in a beautiful garden. Poetry written by women during the Romantic period often referenced domestic scenes.

Like 'The Summer Shower', this poem describes an extreme downpour, concentrating partly on the human reaction and partly on the reaction of nature. The maiden runs to fetch the washing in, covering her 'cap and bows' (2) with her apron, but she is almost 'dowsed … to the skin' (4). The poet describes the downpour in violent terms: the maiden runs away, but she is caught and beaten by the rain.

The next section of the poem describes 'brooks' running through 'ruts' (5), and both the boy and the ploughman have to wade through it, while birds are nearly drowned: 'waded' and 'drowned' are repeated in lines 6–8. The floods cause women to scream when the water comes in at their doors, and working people rush home. The atmosphere of panic is heightened by frequent reference to rushing and hurrying. The poem ends with an image that encapsulates the seriousness of the rain: the 'old stone pit deep as house is high' (13) is full of water, and is possibly the same one that is described in 'Sonnet: "The passing traveller"'.

The brevity of the **sonnet** form adds considerably to its impact. Each line intensifies the scene, and, with the exception of the final **couplet**, Clare constructs each line as if it is self-contained. This gives the poem a lurching rhythm, and emulates a person running away. Listing, one of Clare's frequently used devices, together with the repeated use of 'and', also heightens the sense of accumulating drama.

CHECK THE NET

Further information about the sonnet can be found at **www.sonnets.org**

GLOSSARY

| 5 | **ruts** tracks in the mud road made by wheels |

SONG: 'SHE TIED UP HER FEW THINGS'

- A farm worker prepares to return to her home town when the harvest is almost in.
- The animals and a fellow worker bid her farewell.
- When spring comes, the flowers will miss Jinney's singing.

The poem tells the story of Jinney, who has only a few possessions. One Michaelmas, she takes all that she has and leaves the farm where she works. The animals and the thresher say goodbye in their different ways. Before she leaves, she takes her last look at the farm. Jinney is likely to be back in her own town before the sun is set.

COMMENTARY

The first **stanza** repeats images of tightening, as a woman (whose name we later learn is Jinney) is getting ready to go out. She ties up her possessions, her shoes, and tightens her apron. It is likely that she is an itinerant worker, as she takes her earnings with her. At her departure, the animals all seem to say goodbye to her in their own ways. The thresher stops 'whopping' (14) the floor of the barn, and wishes her good luck. Taking her last look at the 'old mossy farm'

SONG: 'SHE TIED UP HER FEW THINGS' continued

CONTEXT

Michaelmas (29 September) was one of the quarter days when the rent was due and tenancies began and ended. The 'tythes' (21) Clare refers to were a kind of tax (tithe), one tenth of the annual produce or earnings, set aside for the clergy.

(18), she sees the bees buzzing around the thistle, and hears the 'whistle' (17) of the robin. This kind of detailed reference to nature is typical of Clare's poetry.

The final two **stanzas** refer to the time of year. It is autumn – 'Michaelmas season' (19) – the harvest has nearly been brought in, the farmers have finished sharpening their tools, and the doves gather around those who are shelling beans. Next spring, the flowers will miss the woman's singing. The references to her keeping her place in the Bible by turning down the corner of a page and 'her bosom's forewarnings' (28) may hint that she is leaving because of an illness or death in her family. The fact that the harvest has not entirely been brought in may add to the suggestion that she is leaving early for an important reason. The image of the sun setting at the end of the stanza gives a sense of conclusion – both of the **narrative** and of the poem – and is used by Clare in 'Shadows of Taste' and 'Emmonsales Heath'. It also suggests the inevitable turning of time, the harvest year and the seasonal change. Even though Jinney is leaving and will be missed, life on the farm will continue as before.

Clare explores here the idea of home. This is a poignant poem because it is the story of a poor woman who leaves her home; it is also a hopeful poem, as she returns to her own town. The poet identifies himself with the town that Jinney has left, and gives a sense of the loss she will be to those she has left behind by describing her last moments there with vividness.

GLOSSARY

6	**lapped**	put into her lap
10	**prated**	chattered
13	**Thrasher-man**	a thresher; someone who separates grain from straw by beating ('whopping') it
15	**door-cloth**	cloth to keep out draughts
21	**ruckings**	haystacks
22	**Cote**	cottage
	muster	appear
24	**whettings**	sharpenings

THE FODDERING BOY

- A boy folds his arms to keep out the cold while running across the snow.
- The cattle in the field are expecting to be fed, and wait impatiently for the boy's arrival.

An unnamed boy tries to stay warm while rushing through the snow. He is so cold that the wintry wind takes his breath away. When he reaches the place where the hay bales go, he sees the hungry cattle impatiently waiting for him and for the sound he makes when he refills the stack. He places some of the hay on the ground and encourages the cattle to feed.

COMMENTARY

This early poem, dating to 1821–2, is a small **vignette** which presents the essence of a particular farming activity: the feeding of cows. It is typical of Clare's style in that it is an almost photographic representation of a countryside activity. While the description is vivid and detailed, we are given nothing of the boy's inner life or his feelings about the work that he has to do; furthermore, the speaker of the poem reveals little about himself either physically or emotionally. All we know is that he is in a position to observe the scene and is more concerned with the boy's discomfort than any potential discomfort of his own. Clare has removed the **persona** of the speaker in order to focus on the subject of the poem.

The **sonnet** rhymes *abababacacdcdd* and does not seem to have a **volta**. The continuity of the *a* rhyme makes the verse flow, knitting these lines together. The repetition of the 'snows' rhyme echoes the main cause of the cold, but also gives a sense of the verse being bundled up like the boy. It is wrapped up in continuous rhymes like the boy's 'straw-band-belted legs' (2). The final **couplet** and the opening **quatrain** follow the rhyme pattern of the **Shakespearean sonnet**.

 CHECK THE BOOK

William Howard suggests, in *John Clare* (1981), that 'there is no didactic intrusion by the poet; we sense his sympathetic response to what he sees, but he remains outside the scene, content to let the description itself convey his attitude' (p. 110).

CONTEXT

The Shakespearean sonnet, also known as the English sonnet, takes the form of three quatrains with a concluding couplet. The rhyme scheme is usually *abab cdcd efef gg*. Reading this type of sonnet is a little like blowing up a balloon: it gets bigger after each quatrain, and the couplet is the pin that pops it. The volta occurs just before the final couplet.

CHECK THE BOOK

Michael Kramp's article 'The Romantic Reconceptualization of the Gypsy: From Menace to Malleability' (in *Literature Compass* 3:6 (November 2006), pp. 1334–50) explores the cultural history of gypsies. 'Following the hanging of a number of young gypsies at Northampton in 1780, we can trace a slow but notable shift in the English cultural understanding of the itinerant people. While late-eighteenth-century literary texts perpetuate longstanding conceptions of the gypsies as criminals and dangers, early nineteenth-century works construct new images of the gypsies that emphasize their benign alternative lifestyle' (p. 1334).

QUESTION

In what ways, if any, is the poem critical of the gypsy lifestyle? Does Clare suggest any redeeming features?

GLOSSARY

1	**foddering**	bringing or gathering feed
	crumping	making a crunching sound on frozen snow
6	**doublet**	close-fitting jacket
7	**beaver**	hat made of beaver fur
14	**brawls**	makes a noise

THE GIPSY CAMP

- Gypsies make their food over a coal fire in the snow.
- They are regarded by the poet as worthy of sympathy, but they are not romanticised by him.

In this winter scene, the poet paints a picture of an isolated forest in the deep snow which is home to a gypsy camp. The camp has been set up near an oak tree, which serves as a windbreak. The gypsies are cooking some mutton over a coal fire, next to which a dog crouches attempting to get warm and hoping in vain for some food. The poet concludes that this scene is typical of how the gypsies live, and suggests that they are a picturesque and isolated group who steal, and have little protection.

COMMENTARY

Clare presents, in this **sonnet** dating from 1840–1, a brief portrait of a gypsy camp. Clare counted gypsies among his friends, and often visited them on Sundays and on summer evenings, and so draws on his own experiences here. The poem conveys a great deal of sympathy for this 'quiet, pilfering, unprotected race' (14), but also, in a rather contradictory fashion, uses the negative stereotypes that are often seen in literature about them.

Loneliness and isolation are important **themes** in Clare's work, and they are exemplified here. The snow isolates the forest, where the gypsies have set up camp, and a gypsy boy collects wood for the fire. The camp is 'squalid' (5) and cold, but gains some protection from the shelter of an oak tree and bushes. The mutton is bad – 'stinking' (8) – because they are poor, and there is so little to go around that they cannot spare any scraps for the dog. Clare states starkly that this is how they live. Like many of his **vignettes**, this one is described almost as if it is a scene that could be in a painting: 'a picture to the place' (13). Poetry of this type belongs to what is known as the **loco-descriptive** tradition.

The sonnet is unrhymed until the last **couplet**. The unrhymed section gives a sense of the freedom that Clare equates with the gypsy life, and the concluding couplet gives the final statement the air of a judgement. The closing line can be seen as either positive or negative. The gypsies are regarded as thieves, but they are also 'unprotected' (14). This lack of protection may imply that because they are an isolated community, they have few alternatives to theft. Alan Vardy notes that the poem's sole purpose is the 'realistic' depiction of a series of moments, 'the experiences of suffering in the gypsy camp'. Clare is, he argues, not interested in moral judgements (*John Clare, Politics and Poetry*, 2003, p. 27).

THE COTTAGER

- The poet describes an old man who lives in a cottage.
- The cottager's life is regular and monotonous and he is afraid of change.
- He is a man with firm moral views.

The poem is a detailed description of the character of an unnamed cottager who has not been further than fifty miles from home, performs the same activities each day and talks about London as if it is in a foreign land. He is not completely cut off, however. He reads about London in the newspaper, which suggests that he is literate and has some intellectual curiosity.

CHECK THE BOOK

In Jane Austen's *Emma* (1816) Harriet Smith and Miss Bickerton find gypsies threatening when they encounter them on the road. Although the gypsies do nothing, their presence is enough to cause fear. In his poem 'Gipsies' (1807), however, Wordsworth comments: 'In scorn I speak not; – they are what their birth / And breeding suffer them to be; / Wild outcasts of society!' (26–8). John Keats's 'Old Meg' (written in 1818) is in close communion with nature: 'Old Meg she was a gipsy, / And lived upon the moors, / Her bed it was the brown heath turf, / And her house was out of doors' (1–4).

QUESTION

Why do we know so much about this man, yet not know his name?

COMMENTARY

The unnamed cottager in this 1830 character study is a simple man who is stuck in the past – he is **ideologically** conservative. As such, he may be seen as a **symbol** of the slowly changing culture of the countryside. He looks at new advances in technology with scepticism: the steam train seems like 'witchcraft' (12) to him. For him, modern science is as puzzling as the Gothic writing in early printed ('blackletter', 12) books, and he 'views new knowledge with suspicious eyes' (9). While he has not been economically successful, he enjoys life and pays his bills. His trips to the market show that his life is lived in moderation – he only spends an hour there, implying that he does not spend his time drinking.

The cottager is a compassionate person. In spite of the snail mementoes – he keeps 'pooty shells' (94) hanging in wreaths from the cupboards to remind him of his children, who hunted for them while they were young – the cottager does not like any form of hunting, argues vociferously against it, and pleads 'with sad care' (27) for the rights of vermin like foxes and hares. He cares for animals in pain, and 'loudly storms' about 'mad' people (25) who fish. He also feels sorry for people killed in war, even though they are his enemies. Yet while he does not like war, he enjoys the pictures and stories of the British military successes in the imperial war with the French navy. This points to the inconsistency and particularity of his views.

The cottager is also opposed to all kinds of religious enthusiasm (such as that seen in Puritanism and Methodism). His strict moral views mean that he 'deems it sin to sing' a song (33) but not to speak its words. He also prefers **ballads** to be spoken; the old vicar used to recite them, and he takes this vicar to be the authority on this question. He compares the new vicar's sermons with the old vicar's sermons and complains that the new vicar's are full of theology and theological terms that he does not understand. Nevertheless, he still attends church every Sunday. The cottager's old-fashioned attitudes are revealed again by his bowing at the name of Jesus in the liturgy, and his conviction that 'All words of reverence' (49) – such as possessive pronouns referring to God and words like 'lord' – should be spelled with a capital. He has a family Bible which was purchased

CONTEXT

Lines 81–2 are a reference to Admiral George Rodney's victory over the French fleet under the Comte de Grasse in 1872; Lord Robert Manners, the Marquis of Granby's second son, was wounded in the action, and later died.

CONTEXT

The Puritans were an extreme Protestant sect which rejected formal traditions in worship. After the Act of Uniformity (1662) they were known as Dissenters and Nonconformists. The fact that the cottager has a copy of the Book of Common Prayer suggests that he is an Anglican (a member of the Church of England, which was then, as it is now, the established Church in England); his fondness for the vicar also implies this.

by or for his grandfather, and the family has observed the tradition of recording the birth and death dates of its members on the flyleaves.

To the cottager, looking after his household and managing his means (using his homely book on husbandry) is a kind of poetry; he regards verse as frivolous: 'Verse deals in fancy so he sticks to prose' (68). The almanacs and household management books represent the physical – he 'weekly hunts the almanacs for rain' (70) – whereas the religious books belong to the metaphysical world. Even though his education is limited to this, it is quite developed in comparison with that of his neighbours, who 'prize him as the learned man' (72). The reference to the 'tall poplar pointing to the sky' (75) gives us a further idea of the cottager's relationship to nature. He planted it when he was an 'idle boy' (76), and, like him, it is old. It shelters his home, but he is not sentimental about it. He does not have an emotional relationship to nature: 'He hears the mountain storm – and feels it not' (98). In order to practise the husbandry he reads about, he writes down the number of beans in his crop so that he can keep an account of improvements made in his household management. He is content that the cottage chimney is shaded from the wind by the tree, and he is hospitable to his guests. He has decorated his house with natural things: 'the "largest ears of corn" / He ever found his picture frames adorn' (79–80), for example. This character sketch concludes that the cottager is an impregnable individual because mental and physical storms cannot upset him; he is content, and holds his beliefs firmly and sincerely. Clare's larger point may be that the people of the countryside are slow to change their ways, and there is something valuable in that.

 CHECK THE BOOK

The Pilgrim's Progress (1678–84) by John Bunyan (1628–88) tells the story of Christian, who undergoes a number of trials on his way to the Celestial City (an imagined heaven). It was one of the most popular books in the nineteenth century.

CONTEXT

The agricultural poet and writer Thomas Tusser (c.1524–80) first published *A Hundred Good Pointes of Husbandrie* in 1557.

GLOSSARY		
16	**scores**	records of alcohol bought on credit in an alehouse
19–20	**Rover's ... Dapple's**	traditional names for a dog and a horse
86	**Almanac**	an annual table containing a calendar of months and days, with astronomical data and festivals
87	**worsted**	woollen fabric
91	**sedgy**	grassy (coarse grass)

CONTEXT

St Martin's Day, or Martinmas, is the feast of St Martin of Tours and the final day of the farming year (11 November). In England during the medieval and Elizabethan periods it was a festival that involved eating the livestock that could not make it through the winter. Joints of meat were hung in the chimney to dry in order to preserve them; this was called Martinmas beef or mutton.

ST MARTIN'S EVE

- It is winter, and a gathering of people of all ages enjoy an evening party.
- Kate, however, is depressed and lonely because she is a 'fallen' woman.
- The people dance and listen to stories, and eventually go home at midnight.

It is approaching the end of the year, there are no outdoor recreational activities, and the agricultural workers have finished their harvest songs. Abrasive winds have done a great deal of unexpected harm. The birds have flown south and children stay indoors because of the bad weather. Winter evenings indoors, however, have their own pleasures: storytelling, warm wine and late parties. It is St Martin's Eve and there is a very good and boisterous party taking place that is making everyone happy.

While the workers play a number of practical jokes on one another, a woman called Kate is depressed because her heart is broken. She has followed the custom of St Martin's Eve in order to dream of the man she will marry. When the workers have finished dancing, one of them reads stories from a book. They believe every word of the tales because they are in print. The party ends at midnight.

COMMENTARY

The poem concentrates on describing the leisure activities of the people of a rural community, and, as such, links to *The Shepherd's Calendar*. Like 'December', an extract from this 1827 publication, 'St Martin's Eve' is tied to a particular time of year. Although he does not say so here, Clare records the activities in such detail because he believed that they would be lost if they were not described. He laments in 'The Parish' (1820–7), for instance, that children are 'taught at school their stations to despise / And view old customs with disdainful eyes' (153–4).

The poet describes the winding down of the farming year, and the gradual effects of the cold. The descriptions for people and for

CONTEXT

Unpublished during his lifetime, Clare's **satirical** poem 'The Parish' is over two thousand lines long. The line references here and elsewhere refer to the extract quoted in the 1997 Everyman edition used in these Notes.

natural things are interchangeable: the year 'grows wearisome with age' (1) and the children 'fly' (26). The harshness of the weather contrasts with the pleasurable scenes inside the cottage. The practical jokes described all centre on making someone look foolish. The fool or clown (sometimes called Harlequin) appears often in Clare's work; Clare expresses, through his use of the fool, his anxiety over the lack of sophistication of his people. In 'The Author's Address to his Book' (1819) Clare **personifies** a book he has written as a clownish peasant 'lowly bred' (154) whose worth 'will excuse' its 'clownish look' (156). The book contains 'vulgar faults' (157) because its author is uneducated. He hopes that if the 'learned, rich and great' (197) in 'Exalted stations' (165) 'condescend to hear' (167) what he has to say in the book, it may succeed in the literary market. But he 'tremble[s] for thy [the book's] fate' (199) nonetheless.

CHECK THE POEM

Keats's poem 'The Eve of St Agnes' (written in 1819) contains a similar custom concerning a maiden who performs a range of rituals in order to dream about the man she will marry. In Keats's poem the man actually appears in her bedroom.

While 'St Martin's Eve' considers a range of characters, it is interesting because of the way in which it portrays women. Women in John Clare's work generally conform to certain types: gossips, foolish women or the objects of love. They are most often concerned with love, and are frequently 'fallen' women, in the sense that they have had sex before marriage and have either become unmarried mothers or been rejected by all other men because they have lost their reputations. The 'once-beguiled Kate' (113) has lost her reputation, but still has fantasies of falling in love, and hopes to regain her dreams through following the custom of St Martin's Eve. Kate's **melancholy** is self-absorbing. Clare often depicts solitary melancholics in his poems; here, in the second **stanza**, we also have the 'lone and melancholy crane' which is like a 'traveller lost' (17–18). Kate nurses her 'melancholy like a child' (123); this **simile** hints at the reason for her loneliness: she may have lost a child, or it may simply mean that she indulges in her sadness so much that it is as if she is nursing it as a mother. In contrast to Kate, 'Tib a Tinker's daughter' (163), who appears in the tale told within the poem, is an unusual woman in Clare's poetry, as she has ingenuity and is brave. She escapes the witch who holds her captive and, having discovered that she was brave enough to leave, finds better employment elsewhere. Tib represents the underdog overcoming slavery and finding liberty through her own courage.

CONTEXT

Gray (1716–71) is best known for his 'Elegy Written in a Country Churchyard' (published in 1751) and his 'Ode on a Distant Prospect of Eton College'. Regarded as one of the major poets of the eighteenth century, Gray was influenced by the classics, and in turn influenced the Romantic poets, who were particularly drawn to his **melancholic** verse.

CONTEXT

'La Barbe Bleue' ('Bluebeard') was first published by the French author Charles Perrault (1628–1703) in 1697 in a collection of fairy tales which included 'Le Petit Chaperon rouge' ('Little Red Riding Hood'), 'La Belle au bois dormant' ('Sleeping Beauty') and 'Le Chat botté' ('Puss in Boots').

The poem directly references two texts on the **theme** of the pain of knowledge. The quotation '"Where ignorance is bliss 'tis folly to be wise"' (144) is taken from Thomas Gray's 'Ode on a Distant Prospect of Eton College' (written in 1742 and published in 1747). The poem recalls Gray's happy time at Eton, where the ignorance of childhood protected him from the pain of understanding life as an adult. This theme is particularly resonant for Clare, especially in poems such as 'St Martin's Eve' and 'The Parish'. In 'St Martin's Eve' the quotation suggests that the villagers are happy because their horizons are narrow. The other tale mentioned as one that the villagers tell for their entertainment is that of 'Bluebeard' (154), the story of a nobleman who has murdered all of his previous wives. Bluebeard gives a small key to his new young wife and forbids her to open the room it unlocks; while he is away she is overcome with curiosity, opens the door and finds the mutilated bodies of his previous wives. He finds out that she has done this and is about to kill her, when her brothers arrive and kill him. The tale warns that curiosity always leads to pain, and that ignorance is bliss. This may refer to Kate's personal situation, or the joys of the simple life, and it links to the quotation from Thomas Gray.

Geoffrey Chaucer (c.1343–1400) is also mentioned indirectly. The men leaving the party are compared to Chanticleer, who appears in 'The Nun's Priest's Tale' in *The Canterbury Tales* (c.1387). This medieval beast fable tells the story of a cockerel who dreams that he will be attacked by a fox. His wife, Pertelote, dismisses the dream as indigestion, but it turns out to be true. Chanticleer meets the fox, who, appealing to his vanity, convinces him to stretch out his neck and crow with his eyes closed. This recalls one of the practical jokes mentioned in 'St Martin's Eve' (see **stanza** nine). The fox grabs his neck with his teeth, but Chanticleer escapes when the fox attempts to taunt those who are pursuing them. The tale links with Clare's poem in that it is a story about a dream that can predict the future, as the dream of St Martin's Eve is reputed to do. It is also fitting for the description of the drunken men, returning home after the party and bragging.

3	**hinds**	agricultural labourers
4	**Still**	silent
	romp	boisterous play
5	**wont**	was accustomed
7	**mickle**	much
14	**aye**	certain
32	**eldern**	made from elderberries
70	**tittled**	tickled
80	**Slives**	slips quietly in
95	**mash-tub**	tub used in brewing malt
149	**morts**	a great deal of
150	**no stint**	without stopping
186	**younkers**	young men
192	**presage**	foretell or portend

BIRDS AND BEASTS

THE WREN

- Clare wonders why the nightingale and the cuckoo are so popular in literature, when the robin and the wren are just as fascinating.
- The robin and the wren are his personal favourites because of their associations with past memories of home and work.

Clare starts his description of the wren with a question about its cultural significance. He asks why it is less popular as a songbird than the cuckoo or the nightingale. The wren is, he asserts, equally as capable of lifting one's heart joyously, as is the song of the robin. Clare has often shared a hut with this little bird when he has tended the sheep on the plains, and it continues to remind him of happy times.

CONTEXT

Wrens are always referred to as female in folklore and are known by the name Jenny Wren. The bird is considered sacred, and she is regarded as the wife of the robin in British folklore.

COMMENTARY

This **sonnet** (with the rhyme scheme *ababcdcdcdcece*), from *The Midsummer Cushion* collection, begins by asking two questions. The first is unanswered: the poet asks for the reason why cuckoos and nightingales are so popular in poetry. The cuckoo's song is described as a 'melody' (1) and the nightingale's as a 'rich song' (2). The second question is one that the poet answers himself: is there no other bird in nature's choir that often raises the heart to heightened emotion and laughter? By the word 'other' (3), the poet acknowledges that the cuckoo and the nightingale are associated with happiness, but also implies that they have a certain monopoly in the popular imagination. Clare concludes that he does not know how other people form their tastes, but proceeds to explain his own.

Clare uses the word 'caught' (6) to describe how people form their tastes. It is used here in the sense of 'appeal to', as in things that catch the imagination. The word suggests that tastes are formed by passive processes, and are things that catch one and not the other way around. There are, he says, other birds, such as the robin, that 'bear the bell' (7). This means that they can play a tune; but it is also a farming term, meaning 'to take first place' in the flock or herd. These other birds have given him 'crowds of happy memories' (8); the memories are **personified** to make them seem more real and to intensify their significance. Clare is concerned here with memory and place: the birds are precious because they remind him of his former home, and still come to tell him happy stories of the past. He is also concerned with distinguishing himself from the literary tradition, and instead gives an account of the personal significance of the bird. Clare was suspicious of public renown, and preferred to see value as something separate from popularity.

GLOSSARY

4	**minstrelsy**	music or musicians
9	**dell**	valley
13	**Tenting**	attending or watching

SONNET: THE CROW

- The poem expresses the poet's love for crows.

Lonely men find it peaceful to look at a crow flying across a landscape in a wintry March; it reminds them that other people are near by. The poet loves to see them fly past and to hear them croak above the forest and then dodge out of the way of the woodman's axe. He also loves to see a lone crow flying over the landscape.

COMMENTARY

The sonnet moves from the general description of how 'lonely men' (1) see the crow, to how the poet sees the bird. Both descriptions are focused on the crow's relationship to the landscape. Clare suggests that this bird connects lonely people to nearby communities, because it flies so far and is present where there is food to scavenge and so where there are people. The sadness of the lonely men is emphasised by the wintry weather.

Like 'The Wren', this poem is about redirecting the literary tradition away from its usual associations. Traditionally the crow is unlucky, and is a **symbol** of discord; in Clare's poem, however, it is a symbol of peace and of connection. The repetition of 'I love' (7, 11 and 13) adds to this positive portrait. The crow, from its vantage point, can see things that are inaccessible to people, and this omniscient perspective makes it seem a symbol of hope. It is also associated with happiness. Its 'croaking joy' (12) is unexpected, since croaking is usually associated with illness or sadness. Clare also links the crow to happiness in 'The Crow Sat on the Willow'.

Clare picks out the colour of the birds as a focus. They are likened to 'chimney-sweeps' (7) covered in soot, but this is not a sad image for the poet. He introduces **picturesque imagery** in the description of the forest as 'gnarled' (8). The bird is in harmony with the woodman's chopping, flying out of the way in time to miss his axe. We see nature and mankind in harmony in the two wood images: the March wind tears 'off the branches of the huge old oak' (6) and the woodman chops wood in the forest. The woodman is another of

CHECK THE POEM

Clare's 'Sonnet: "I love to hear the evening crows go by"' also expresses the poet's love of the sound that the crow makes. More recently, Ted Hughes wrote a sequence of poems entitled *Crow* (1970).

CONTEXT

Jacqueline Simpson and Steve Roud note, in *A Dictionary of English Folklore* (2000), that crows are 'generally regarded as unlucky, and as omens of death, especially if they croak persistently near a house, or fly low over its roof'.

CONTEXT

Franz Schubert (1797–1828) set Wilhelm Müller's poem 'Die Krähe' ('The Crow') to music in a song cycle entitled *Winterreise* (*Winter Journey*) in 1827–8. Here the crow is a **symbol** of death; it accompanies the singer on his journey, waiting for him to die so that it can feed on him. The singer says that the crow will not have to wait long, and sees its persistence as a fiendish kind of loyalty.

Clare's solitary characters; his 'stroke' is 'hid' (9), implying that he is hidden and separate from the human world.

The perspective of the poet changes in the last two lines: the first of these suggests that he observes the crow from below, the second that he is with the crow in imagination looking down on the landscape 'spread below' (14). The fluidity and ease with which the poet moves around this landscape echoes the freedom and movement of the bird.

GLOSSARY

1	**peaceable**	peaceful
3	**fen**	lowlands covered with shallow water
4	**nigh**	near
9	**sosh**	dip in flight
10	**ply**	bend

THE SKYLARK

- The poet imagines that boys collecting flowers are fantasising about being skylarks.
- Despite the skylark's soaring flight, the bird's nest is hidden away at ground level.

In early spring, boys compete to pick the best flowers; and the skylark flies through the air, singing. She returns to the nest, which the boys pass without noticing. It is quite low to the ground, which they would never guess was the case. If the boys could fly as high, Clare argues they would build nests in the clouds and travel the world.

COMMENTARY

Dated between 1825 and 1826, 'The Skylark' is a poem about youthful ambition and imagination. The poet is fascinated by the skylark and by the boys who are listening to it, and he connects them in his mind by imagining that they are wishing for the skylark's ability to fly. The boys are imaginative in other ways too, he observes. They are especially excited to find buttercups, which are precious 'golden caskets' (10).

The poet sets the scene carefully. It is early spring and the skylark has not finished building her nest. The ploughing instruments are unused because all the crops have been planted and the corn is beginning to sprout. It is a warm March day, and boys have wandered far from home to pick spring flowers, competing to find the first one. While they run, the skylark swoops up, and the swish it makes is compared to the sound of winnowing. The harvesting image links to that of the boys harvesting flowers.

Danger features in the poem in two ways. The terrified young hare at the beginning of the poem is camouflaged as a 'brown clod' (6) of earth, while the poet imagines the concern of the boys as they contemplate building nests of their own in the sky (22–4). The boys' anxiety about safety links to the scene with the bull in 'The Summer Shower' (65–72). They do not want the life of the hare, but wish to be 'As free from danger as the heavens are free / From pain and toil' (23–4). Here the heavens can be seen as a **metaphor** for the exploration of the boys' elevated imagination. The poem seems to imply, however, that while the bird soars to these great heights, she is unwise in nesting at ground level, 'where any thing / May come at to destroy' the nest (19–20). The human condition, here **symbolised** by the attitude of the boys who want to soar high and assume that height equates to safety, is contrasted with nature, and the unexpected nesting behaviour of the skylark, who finds real safety near the ground.

Like 'The Wren' and 'Sonnet: The Crow', this poem exists within a literary context. Percy Bysshe Shelley published a poem called 'To a Skylark' in 1820. Like Clare's bird Shelley's skylark sings in the clouds, and Shelley's poem is about aspiration. The skylark, for Shelley, stands for the perfect and happy production of art. The 'blithe' (1) bird pours out its 'full heart / In profuse strains of unpremeditated art' (5). The final five lines of Clare's poem contain elevated language of the type that can be seen in Shelley's. 'O were they but a bird' (26) is spoken both from the perspective of the poet

 CHECK THE POEM

Many of Clare's poems feature boys actively searching for the eggs of wild birds, or imply that boys are a threat to nests. Clare regarded bird's-nesting as removing beauty and song from the world (see 'The Nightingale's Nest'). The boy in 'Sonnet: "The passing traveller"' is in search of a magpie's eggs, and the pettichap in 'The Summer Shower', with her nest similarly close to the ground, is oblivious to the threat of bird's-nesting boys.

CONTEXT

One of the major poets of the Romantic era, Shelley was educated at Eton and Oxford and was an intellectual and political radical who argued that the poet figure (or creator) was at the heart of society.

and from the boys, and is therefore free indirect speech. Clare uses this linguistic form in order to highlight the potential excitement that the boys would feel.

> **GLOSSARY**
>
> 1   **rolls** horse-drawn roller for ploughing
>
>   **harrows** heavy frames with sharp teeth used for ploughing
>
> 3   **clods** solid lumps of earth
>
> 4   **spiry** pointing like a spire
>
> 14   **Winnows** exposing grain to the air in order to separate waste particles from it
>
> 17   **unheeding** disregarding
>
> 30   **leveret** a young hare in its first year

SONNET: 'AMONG THE ORCHARD WEEDS'

- An old hen causes a nuisance by laying her eggs in random places.
- Both a servant girl and a young boy search in vain for the eggs.

An old hen makes her nest from the weeds found in the orchard; her cackle alerts the servant girl that there are eggs to collect. She wanders all over the orchard looking for the eggs, but in vain. A boy hopes to find the hen and her eggs in the haystack, and is surprised, one Sunday, to find that the eggs have hatched.

COMMENTARY

As with several of Clare's nest poems, the comfort of the nest is emphasised: 'Snugly and sure' (2). This sonnet is concerned with the humorous situation of the nest that cannot be found – humorous because this is a domestic bird, and the nest is meant to be accessible. The servant is forced to hunt for the eggs and suffer the annoyance of being stung by nettles. The hen's 'cackling' (8) is almost like ridicule, and the word 'still' (8) implies that the servant has been trying to encourage the hen to lay her eggs in more conventional places. The poem resolves with an unexpected turn of events: hatched chicks 'come chirping to the door' (14). The **rhyming couplet** emphasises that this is the conclusion of the tale.

> **GLOSSARY**
>
> 8   **pullet** a young hen

THE LANDRAIL

- It is summertime and the poet hears the mysterious landrail's song, but it is hard to place where the sound is coming from.
- It is a bird that people then knew little about, and was only discovered during harvest.
- The landrail (or corncrake) lays its eggs in holes in wheat fields.

The poet remarks that the landrail's song is a common sound in summer, although it is an elusive bird which is difficult to get close to. Boys, who are knowledgeable about birdsong, 'wonder at' (24) its song and cannot find the bird. Yet it is not rare; it stays relatively close at hand but always hidden, and lays its eggs in the wheat field.

COMMENTARY

The poet sets the scene in the opening **stanza**, and describes the pleasant summer fields and mentions that the landrail is calling out during the 'weeding time' (5). The corn is waving 'knee deep' (6) and the weeders are working in the fields. The poet moves from a collective experience: 'We hear it' (5) to an individual experience: 'And now I hear it' (9). The poem is typical of Clare's use of time. In the third stanza a minute passes between lines 11 and 12. Again, he gives a sense of a tightening focus as we move from the collective experience to the individual experience and from the vast expanse of time to the small minute.

Landrails sing in the summer grass, which is long and pleasant and keeps them hidden from view. Although its song is heard, the bird is difficult to place, and as such becomes a **symbol** of uncertainty. There is possibly a religious point being made here too. The bird seems to be omnipresent, but is nowhere tangible – this makes it

 CHECK THE NET
The Royal Society for the Protection of Birds (RSPB) has a picture of a landrail (also known as a corncrake) on its website and a recording of its song: visit **www.rspb.org.uk** and search for 'corncrake'.

seem like God. Perhaps Clare is interested in the impossibility of the totality of perception – we can feel reality around us, but we cannot grasp it in its entirety. The religious idea is reinforced by the word 'mystery' (57), which is used to describe the bird. **Paradoxically**, Clare can recognise the bird, which gives him a privileged position as someone initiated into the mystery, and who is more at one with nature than he is with human society.

THE NIGHTINGALE'S NEST

- Even though the poet has grown up, he still searches for the nightingale's nest as if he were a boy.
- We find the nest with him and he identifies himself with the solitude of the bird.

We are invited to visit a woodland which has in the past been frequented by nightingales, and Clare observes that the bird, although very plain to look at, has the sweetest song. He imagines that she is happy in 'her home of love' (4) and that the thrush is envious of this happiness. The poet asks us to be quiet as the nightingale can now be heard. We are in search of her secret nest and are requested to part the branches in order to find it. Our presence disturbs the bird, and the poet decides that it is time to leave as we have scared her so much that she is now silent. He asks her to carry on singing and hopes that her nest will not be harmed. Because the nest is hard to find, the poet identifies the nightingale as a lover of solitude.

COMMENTARY

Two key elements distinguish this poem: firstly the personal connection the poet feels with the nightingale; secondly the privileged and direct way we are invited to follow the poet on his journey: 'let's softly rove' (1). The poem opens with an image of a boundary, one of Clare's most common features. He invites us to close the gate softly as we pass into the wood. This **symbolises** moving into a different realm, and the beginning of a new and interesting experience. The poet is alert to noise from the beginning as his presence signals danger for the bird and could put an end to what he is looking for – the

 CHECK THE NET
Read Ronald Blythe's 'The Poet and the Nest' at **www.vam.ac.uk** – search for the author and title. This short extract from Blythe's longer study *A Writer's Day-Book* (2006) discusses the importance of nests in Clare's work.

nightingale's song. There is, then, a fragility to the experience. He stresses the familiarity of this experience, nevertheless, as it resurrects similar memories from his childhood.

The vividness and specificity of the description makes the present and the past seem intertwined, and so the child with the bluebells (in the present) is laughing and creeping in the place where he 'did … many hours employ' (15), and where we now are. Clare stresses the cyclical side of nature and includes himself in the comparison: 'I hunted like a very boy' (12). Where the bluebell child hunts for flowers, Clare has hunted for the nightingale's nest. Hunting as a recreation implies destruction, but there is no destruction intended on the part of the poet. The image of the hunt is used because the poet, like a predator, has to be silent in order to find the bird. Thus Clare contrasts the benign aim of the birdwatcher's search with the malignity of the hunter's approach. He often compares his own respect for nature with a disrespect he sees in others in order to promote his preservationist views.

Clare compares the hidden nest with a 'thought unborn' (16). The comparison indicates that the nest is so private, it is as if it is contained in the mind; Clare intensifies this comparison by suggesting that it is even more private than a thought – it is like a thought that has not yet been made. Clare is more than happy to put up with some discomfort to see the bird, and we enter the wild countryside by creeping through thorns. The forest, in myths and legends such as Jacob and Wilhelm Grimm's fairy tales, is always a place of trial. Clare was interested in these tales, and may have been thinking of the difficult access to the nest as a trial by thorns. The bird too is 'Lost in a wilderness of listening leaves' (32). While trying to find her, and to put himself at the same level as the bird, the poet nestles down – it is as if he is creating his own nest – to watch her while she sings. This is the beginning of Clare's **anthropomorphising** of the natural world in this poem. He expresses the similarity between himself and the bird: they both have to hide. She will only sing if she cannot hear him, and she can only be seen if she cannot see him. This parallels Clare's own attitude to writing poetry; anonymity was his preferred state, and so the bird stands as a **symbol** for the anonymous artist, removed from the world of poetic fame and enveloped in nature.

CONTEXT

'Little Red-Cap', or 'Rotkäppchen', appeared in the Brothers Grimm collection in 1812. This tells the story of a young girl who meets a wolf in a forest. The wolf eats the girl's grandmother, and then dresses up in her grandmother's clothes and eats the girl. A huntsman opens up the wolf and finds her there, and Little Red Riding Hood learns never to stray from the path in the forest again. The earliest written version of this folk tale is Charles Perrault's 'Le Petit Chaperon rouge', published in 1697.

Clare sets aside the classical heritage of the bird, as does Samuel Taylor Coleridge (1772–1834) in 'The Nightingale' (1798). For both poets the bird stands for joy rather than the **melancholy** of the classical tradition. Clare also dissociates the bird from her association with night. He recognises that this is a famous bird, but she is not meant to be seen – her dress is only plain brown. It is possible to conclude that he **anthropomorphises** her by referring to her 'dress' (21) and her 'ecstasy' (22), though this can be seen in another light: dress can mean general appearance, and he says that her feathers stand on end 'as 'twere with joy' (23) – her response is like joy, but is not joy itself. She makes the poet 'happy' (27) and so is a **symbol** of happiness from his perspective. His repetition of the word 'happy' may **allude** to John Keats's poem 'Ode to a Nightingale' (published in 1820). The thrush is envious of the nightingale's song. The reason for the thrush's inferiority is that it stays in Britain during the winter and so has 'cares' (36) or troubles. The nightingale flies south for the winter, and so is always happy: 'Her joys are evergreen' (41).

CHECK THE POEM

William Cowper's poem 'Yardley Oak' (written in 1791, published in 1804) describes an ancient oak tree as 'A shattered veteran, hollow-trunked' (4). Wordsworth refers to oaks very frequently.

The conversational **tone** of the poem is highlighted by the exclamation 'Hark!' at line 42; and the poet includes the reader in the experience more directly by telling us to be quiet in order that we do not disturb the bird. He sees the bird sitting on the branch of an old oak, but she is quiet because she is frightened, and the joy that she usually expresses has gone. Clare is making the point here that the presence of people changes the emotions of the bird and destroys her beauty, because the beauty is in her song. She only becomes melancholy through human presence: 'For from man's haunts she seemeth nought to win' (82). She lives in a wild and lonely place because she has nothing to gain from her contact with people – they make her mute with fear. To steal her eggs is to take away the music that the baby birds will make when they grow up: in the last line Clare will call them 'the old woodland's legacy of song' (93) – the next generation of singers. The nightingale is encouraged by the poet to sing on, because it seems as if music is hidden in every flower – that is, the surrounding plants are made musical by her. Clare plays on the musical reference in 'harebells' (72), and imagines that they bow their heads in song. The 'gaping cuckoo' plant (74) is also anthropomorphised; it can hear the song and it seems to blush like a boy looking at a pretty girl. The love

imagery is implied in the way that the bird is serenading the plants; in return, the bowing flowers exhibit courteous behaviour.

The descriptions of the nightingale's nest in this poem are intriguing. It is made from a mixture of noble and common building materials; the moss is like 'velvet' (79), but the grass is in 'scraps' (80). Again this emphasises that the beauty of the nightingale is in her song and not in her creative actions or appearance, but also hints at a **personification** of nature as a 'builder' (83). Nature constructs comfortable homes for her children (the poet is possibly referring to both himself and the bird here) even in places which are remote from people: 'Where solitude's disciples spend their lives' (85). The bird is like a hermit, hidden from and uncontaminated by human society, and her nest is snug. Clare too sees himself as a poet of solitude, and, like the bird, finds his voice in lonely places away from the interference of people.

GLOSSARY

17	**crimping**	wrinkling
	ramp	romp or grow luxuriously
42	**Hark**	listen
54	**stulp**	stump
72	**harebells**	bellflowers with pale blue flowers

THE YELLOWHAMMER'S NEST

- The poet observes a yellowhammer frightened by a young boy.
- Its birdsong is equated to writing poetry.
- The nest is a happy place until snakes take the young.

Near to a wooden bridge, the bird is frightened by a young cowherd. The poet invites us to search for the nest, and we find it easily, on the bank of a shallow brook. It contains five eggs, and Clare likens the yellowhammer to a poet. We leave the nest happy, but we are warned that misfortune visits even happy places. Snakes eat the young and the birds mourn this loss deeply.

 QUESTION

In another of his poems about birds, 'Little Trotty Wagtail', Clare gives the bird a name. What effect does this have?

COMMENTARY

The poem, written in 1825–6, begins *in medias res* (in the middle of things) and, as is usual for Clare's poetry, is situated in a very specific landscape that is described in detail. The poet invites the reader to hunt for the nest of the yellowhammer, in the fashion of his poem 'The Nightingale's Nest'. Again the nest is low down, and we are invited to stoop with him. The search is full of hazards, but we are reassured that we do not need to be frightened: the brook is 'scarcely deep enough a bee to drown' (5). We find the nest – 'Aye, here it is' (7) – close to the bank, underneath the long grass.

It is a roughly built nest, made of faded grass taken from the cornfields. In it are five eggs, and they look as if they have been written on with a scratchy pen. He imagines – 'fancy' (14) – that the eggs have poetry written on them, and magical spells associated with the countryside. The yellowhammer is, then, a kind of poet; and like a nature poet she lives among the weeds and flowers. A link to classical poets is made as the bird's mate sits on a molehill that reminds Clare of the mountain Parnassus, which was sacred to the Muses. Theirs is a happy home full of sunshine, flowers and streams; yet even though it is a kind of paradise, it is not completely protected from harm. Snakes, like an annoying weed that is common everywhere, hunt for the eggs. The harm that they do is as devastating as the damage done by the plague, as is conveyed in the **simile** in line 27. The nest is a 'houseless home' (28), because it is a home, but there is no house, only a nest. The reaction of the birds is grief; they mourn, their hearts are broken, and they are thus **anthropomorphised**. Clare may be **alluding** here to the Garden of Eden and the Fall of Man, as described in the Bible's Book of Genesis (see Chapter 3 for an account of the serpent that enters paradise and destroys the happiness there).

GLOSSARY		
1	**brig**	bridge
3	**dewberry**	a kind of blackberry
24	**noisome**	annoying
	burthens	burdens

SONNETS: THE HEDGEHOG

- Clare describes the nesting, foraging and natural habitat of the hedgehog.
- He laments the lot of the hedgehog, which, even though it does little harm, is hunted by gypsies for meat.

The scene is set in autumn: the hedge is rotting and there are crab apples on the ground. The hedgehog is not a solitary animal; many passers-by stoop down and look at him. The gypsies think that the creature's meat is sweet, but Clare finds it 'bitter and unsavoury' (14). It is believed that the hedgehogs steal the milk from cows, but Clare says that this is impossible. Farmers train shepherd dogs to hunt the hedgehog; Clare, however, is sympathetic towards the animal.

COMMENTARY

Clare links together two **sonnets** to create a compact poem that focuses on the hedgehog and the gypsies, and the way in which they interact. The first sonnet sets up the portrait of a harmless animal which makes a large nest that is an attractive sight for passers-by. The hedgehog's harmless nature is stressed by words like 'hides' (1), 'creep away' (6) and 'whistles' (10). Clare contrasts this with the aggression of the gypsies who 'hunt it with their noisy dogs' (12). Here he seems to show a less sympathetic portrait of the gypsies than is seen in 'The Gipsy Camp', emphasising their difference from other people and the harm they cause. The knowledge that Clare possesses of the habitat and nesting habits of the hedgehog contrasts with the mythology that the gypsies associate with the animal. He regards the belief that they can suck milk from cows as irrational given the empirical evidence. Their mouths are simply too small. The two sonnets are closely linked through their repeated words 'call it sweet' (13 and 16), 'hedge[s]' (1 and 25), 'hog' (11 and 21), 'dog[s]' (12, 22 and 26) and 'rotten' (1 and 15).

GLOSSARY

9	**crabs**	crab apples
	sloes	wild berries

CHECK THE BOOK

John Goodridge and Kelsey Thornton call the gypsies Clare's 'natural allies' and suggest that, as 'users of common land, maintaining its status as a sanctuary, in an increasingly enclosed landscape', they held a shared interest with Clare ('John Clare: the trespasser' in *John Clare in Context*, edited by Hugh Haughton, Adam Phillips and Geoffrey Summerfield, 1994, pp. 103–4).

CHECK THE POEM

William Cowper calls gypsies 'A vagabond and useless tribe' (559) in Book I of *The Task* (published in 1785), suggesting that they eat 'Their miserable meal' (561) of 'flesh obscene of dog, / Or vermin, or, at best, of cock purloined' (563–4). Cowper criticises slavery in the same poem, but his tolerance does not extend as far as gypsies.

SONNET: 'I FOUND A BALL OF GRASS AMONG THE HAY'

- The poet finds a nest that he assumes belongs to a bird.
- It belongs, however, to a mouse that is feeding her young.
- The poet is surprised and disgusted by the sight.

The poet finds a ball of grass among the hay and pokes it as he passes by, thinking there might be a bird inside and hoping to catch it. Instead a mouse appears, with her young attached to her teats, and the poet is disturbed by the sight. Unusually for Clare, he has a bad reaction to the nest and runs away, wondering what it could be. He rustles nearby weeds and the mouse flees, abandoning her squeaking young ones.

COMMENTARY

This is a poem about expectations: the poet expects one experience and is forced to encounter another. It is also a poem about femininity: Clare is confronted by the image of a female mouse feeding her young and is alarmed by it. This should be a natural scene, but, because he has scared the creature, the mouse bolts out from the nest with her young still 'hanging at her teats' (6). This is, then, not an image of comfort or nourishment, but one of fear, and the poet seems to be as scared as the mouse. Clare describes his confusing and indecisive actions: he 'ran' (8), and yet he 'pushed' (9) away the weeds to have another look. The mouse is as frightened as the nightingale in 'The Nightingale's Nest', and she scurries away, only returning after the intrusive poet has departed. The poet's main reactions are surprise and disgust. The creature is incongruous in that it looks old, but is feeding a litter of babies.

In the final **couplet**, the scene moves away from the pile of hay where the nest is to a stream which appears to be dry, and has left behind glittering pools. The description of the setting after the event is unexpected (one might assume that the setting would be at the beginning of the poem). The incongruity of this reversal seems to reflect the other surprise of the poem – the ugliness of the scene of the nursing mouse, which should be a comforting sight.

QUESTION

Clare's poem 'Sonnet: "One day when all the woods were bare"' has a very similar subject as Clare is surprised to discover a squirrel in what he thought was a bird's nest. How do the two poems compare?

GLOSSARY	
2	**progged** poked or prodded
9	**knapweed** a common weed with light purple flowers
14	**cesspools** pools of water that gather when the river is low

THE ANTS

- The poet wonders whether ants have a developed social, political and linguistic system that may link them to a fairy era of the past.

Clare suggests that curious people looking at the activities of an ant colony will wonder whether they have a government and laws of their own, because their world seems so ordered. He gives an example of this ordered lifestyle, observing that some ants watch others work, and suggests that these ants encourage the labourers. He also observes something that he finds more incredible: ants cooperate with each other when they engage in a difficult task that one or two ants alone could not achieve efficiently. Clare supposes that ants must have linguistic capabilities, though their language is obviously not audible to humans. Their practices suggest, perhaps, that they have a political and legal system which ensures such cooperation. He imagines that they have laws which have been passed to them from a time when fairies existed.

COMMENTARY

The poem links to a cultural tradition that supposes that ants have a sophisticated society that echoes human civilisation. This tradition goes back to Aristotle (384–322 BC), who observed in *Politics* that ants appear to act cooperatively in ways that foster their survival as a group, and thus that they count as political animals. Aristotle made the same observation about bees, using the example of ants and bees to argue that political – and therefore human political – society is natural, rather than being necessarily the result of a voluntary agreement (as in modern democratic theories, which suppose that political society requires an agreement or contract between citizens). Aristotle thought that, in the ideal world, a state would be a

CHECK THE POEM

Anthropomorphised insects and animals are not uncommon in Clare's work. The landrail is 'Right glad to meet the evening's dewy veil' (13) in 'Summer Moods'; the crow is 'in love' (31) in 'The Crow Sat on the Willow'; and the robin 'sighed but kissed me not' (18) in 'Ballad: "I dreamt not what it was to woo"'. See also 'The Yellowhammer's Nest' and 'The Nightingale's Nest' for further examples.

CONTEXT

According to Aristotle's *History of Animals* some animals are solitary, and some live in communities and are therefore political. Ants, bees, wasps and humans are all political animals because they can combine forces to fulfil a task. Aristotle argues, in his *Politics*, that humans are more political than animals because of their capacity for reasoned speech.

monarchy, although he believed, in the actual world, government was best operated by a larger number of people acting together. The poet seems to admire the world of the ants, suggesting that its sophistication warrants amazement. Their language is 'Too fine for us to hear' (12), suggesting that it is quiet, but 'fine' may also imply that the language is too good or sophisticated for us to hear. The poem highlights how little we know about nature – 'in ignorance we muse' (3) – even from empirical observation. The natural world is also often linked to a **golden age** or Eden, also known in classical mythology as Arcadia. Here the 'fairy days' (14) stand in place of Eden as a kind of pagan paradise of order and cooperation.

LOVE

FIRST LOVE'S RECOLLECTIONS

- Clare suggests that he will never forget his first love.
- Time has, however, changed everything between them.
- When they last parted, they did not think that it would be for ever.

In this poem Clare risks the anger of his first love, Mary, by thinking back to the times when they were together. He remembers how they used to hate being apart; now they have been apart for nine years and he cannot see her clearly in his dreams. He is embarrassed to confess that he still loves her; he is certain, however, that impressions linger on, and this may mean that she retains some tender feelings towards him. Before he became a public poet, his life was simpler, and her praise of his poetry was important to him. When they last said goodbye to each other, he little thought that it would mean parting for ever.

COMMENTARY

It makes sense to read this poem biographically because the poet mentions his love by name, and we can assume her to be Mary Joyce. The poem also dates to 1825, nine years after their relationship had ended. The poem sustains a comparison,

CHECK THE BOOK

Roger Sales notes, in *John Clare: A Literary Life* (2002), that 'Clare criticism has always been attuned to the way in which he creates golden ages and lost Edens: the landscapes of his childhood; the love that may have been possible for a time with Mary Joyce' (p. 137).

CONTEXT

Clare met Mary Joyce (1797–1838), the daughter of a local farmer, at the age of twelve in Glinton while he was at school (see Clare's poem 'Glinton Spire'). Their relationship ended in 1816, probably because her family saw Clare as an unsuitable match, yet his feelings for her remained strong throughout his life. Mary died, unmarried, at the age of forty-one.

throughout, between love and the lives of flowers and plants. The first **stanza** comments that the emotional experience of falling in love for the first time and losing that love is akin to smelling a 'frail rose' (3) that retains its 'fragrance' (4) until it dies. The stem of a plant that has blossomed in summer (the first love) is the basis on which the next blossom is to emerge (the next love).

The poem has much to say about the role of poetry too. In writing to Mary so publicly, Clare is concerned that he will 'vex' her 'ear' (11) with his 'idle song' (12). Time and change have 'not blotted out' (13) his former love; here Clare uses a **metaphor** associated with writing: time does not cross out his words. Once again we see Clare's preference for privacy and genuine praise: her love and praise were better than any public approval. Their mutuality is seen in her embarrassment at hearing his verses: 'Thy blushing look of ready praise' (59) – they are embarrassed together. Now he is concerned that her 'fervent love' (61) has turned to 'scorn severe' (62). The songs that others enjoy are, he supposes, discordant to her.

Stanza three is explicitly concerned with the mouth. Having talked about singing to her in the previous stanza, Clare remembers their speech, 'When honied tokens from each tongue' (17) told each other how they loved. Their words were as sweet as honey, and Clare 'clung' (19) to Mary's lips, while she smiled at him. Her bodily reaction would be very different now, he fears: if his mouth whispered in her ear she would startle like a wild bird and blush. His embarrassment at admitting publicly that he still loves her makes it seem as if his words are themselves alive and blushing: 'My words e'en seem to blush for shame' (43). They have been apart so long now, he cannot accurately recollect Mary's face. His 'very dreams forget' (37) how beautiful she was, but he knows that she is beautiful, though she is a stranger to him.

Clare uses a balanced line in stanza four to show how mutual their relationship was: 'How loath to part, how fond to meet' (25), and his sadness at its loss dominates the central stanzas. He reduces his impression of their current relationship, strangers, to the issue of her possible reaction to his name. The name stands for the essence of the man here, and he supposes that she might be making fun of him. The poem ends with their farewell to each other. It was goodbye,

CONTEXT

Clare's autobiographical fragments also recall his love for Mary: 'she was a beautiful girl and as the dream never awoke into reality her beauty was always fresh in my memory' (*John Clare: By Himself*, edited by Eric Robinson and David Powell, 2002, p. 87).

CHECK THE POEM

Clare's poem 'My Mary' is worth looking at in this context.

but it was not intended as a final farewell. Mary had pretended to say goodbye – he heard her 'feign adieu' (66) – and they expected to see each other again. Clare concludes with the flower **metaphor**, suggesting that their love was like one of the many spring buds that do not mature into a flower.

> **GLOSSARY**
>
> | 57 | **Ere** before |
> | 58 | **meed** reward |

SONG: 'SAY WHAT IS LOVE'

- The poet explores the nature of love and finds it hard to define.

Clare raises the question of the **paradoxical** nature of love. Is it the paradox of alternating between life and death, between rejection and acceptance? Is it the paradox of being imprisoned at the same time as being free? Is it to be alone and to wait hopelessly for what you think is true love? The poet then suggests that love is transient, and concludes that, whatever love is, its centre is focused on his Mary.

COMMENTARY

In another poem about his love for Mary Joyce, Clare asks whether true love exists and describes its intangibility. Love is like a 'sunbeam on the mist' (8), fading into nothing, never to be replaced or experienced again; it is like a blossoming rose that fades like temporary fame. If we suppose that the poet is referring to his own fame, then this suggests that he feels cheated that it is now gone, and that fame turned out to be as fleeting as love, **symbolised** here by the rose petal, the rose being a traditional **symbol** for love (Clare makes a **pun** on the 'leaf' of the book and the rose leaf here). He uses the image of fading for the rose and the sunbeam in order to stress the difficulty of attaching a meaningful definition to love. This image also appears in the first **stanza** of 'First Love's Recollections'.

QUESTION

How does Clare's use of language in this poem describe the elusive quality of love?

The form of the poem is deceptively simple. It is written in **rhyming couplets** and in **iambic tetrameter**. The ideas are complex, but the verse form is straightforward. Several of the lines contain a **caesura** – a pause indicated by a dash. This line division emphasises that the question being raised in the first half of the line is answered in the second. The answers, however, take longer than half a line to complete, again emphasising the difficulty of defining love. Its complexity is seen in the powerful effect that this simplicity has. Clare is able to grapple with huge and complex questions concerning his emotional landscape using a simple vocabulary and a simple poetic form.

> **GLOSSARY**
>
> 10   **o'ertook** encountered
> 11   **blooming** blossoming
> 12   **leaf** petal

BALLAD: 'THE SPRING RETURNS, THE PEWIT SCREAMS'

- Clare laments the loss of his love, Mary, and is reminded of her by the piercing cry of the peewit.
- The bird was praised by Mary once, when he pledged his heart to her.
- She is now estranged from him, and he is still heartbroken.
- From this he makes the bitter generalisation that all women are unreliable.

The poet declares that spring is returning and that he can hear the peewit's loud cry, indicating that this is so. Near a local bridge Mary 'praised the screaming plover' (10) – another name for the peewit – and he told her that he loved her, giving her a daisy as a token of his love. Later she rejected him because of his poverty. The peewit screams now, but Mary is no longer with him and Clare has no hope of winning her love again. He concludes that women are as changeable as the wind.

 CHECK THE NET
The RSPB website has further information on the peewit – visit **www.rspb.org.uk** and search for 'lapwing'.

COMMENTARY

Dating from between 1819 and 1832, this **ballad** recalls the breakdown of the relationship between Clare and Mary Joyce. It shares much with 'First Love's Recollections', in that it compares their past intimacy with their current estrangement. The poem suggests that she has married someone else – 'Another name she owns' (39) – but in real life Mary did not marry, and she died in a fire in 1838, after Clare had been admitted to the asylum. Clare may have been told about her death, but he believed her to be alive, and during spells of madness thought himself to have been married to her.

The poem, written in a **stanza** form used in ballads, with the rhyme scheme *abab*, is a simple tale of intense love and betrayal. The happiness of experiencing nature is linked to the happiness of love, through the song of the peewit and the delight that the lovers feel in spring. Clare refers to the May Day celebration at the beginning of the poem; here he suggests that a garland of flowers was displayed. These were often large and elaborately woven, and he compares the simple beauty of one daisy with this collection of specially chosen flowers, finding the daisy more to his taste. Clare often highlights oddities and incongruities in nature – for example he is struck by the grotesqueness of the nursing mouse in 'Sonnet: "I found a ball of grass among the hay"' – and here he highlights the harshness of the peewit's song. We can, perhaps, read its scream as an omen for the demise of the relationship; it is a terrifying presence within a beautiful scene.

Clare uses a collection of images concerned with wealth and value. The daisy, a **symbol** of their love, was once as precious as gold (19) to Mary. He sold the blossom for the price of a kiss, and believed himself to be as rich as a king as a consequence. His throne was in Mary's 'bosom' (24) because it was in her heart. He reflects that he little thought, at this time of complete happiness, that an 'evil hour' (25) was almost upon him. He characterises this troubled time through the **metaphor** of a storm: 'an evil hour / Was bringing clouds around me' (25–6). Clare describes himself, momentarily, as Christlike in his suffering, the flower of love unexpectedly becoming the thorn that wounded him. Mary showed him the withered flower, yet its withered state did not **symbolise** the decline

CONTEXT

Clare writes that peewits 'make no nest but use a horse footing or any hollow they can find they lay four eggs of an olive green color splashed with large black spots and the narrow points ... are always laid inwards they have a way of decoying any thing from their young or nest by swopping [pouncing] and almost tumbling over before them as if wounded and going to fall uttering their harsh screaming note but when near the nest they are silent' (*John Clare's Birds*, edited by Eric Robinson and Richard Fitter, 1982, pp. 83–4).

of the relationship, at this point, but suggested that the token was so precious that it was to be preserved. Nevertheless, by the end of the fourth stanza, Mary 'leaned to wealthy praise' (31), suggesting that the poet is no longer her lover because of his poverty. Clare's love is 'poor' (32), and Mary is his 'stolen treasure' (40).

The poem concludes with musings on the difference between closeness in physical terms and closeness in emotional terms. Mary seems far away emotionally, even though in reality she would have been only an hour's journey away. Clare turns to the familiar metaphor that he associates with distress: the sea. If roaring seas parted them physically, they could not be further apart than they are emotionally. Clare's final observation is a generalisation about the behaviour of women. He suggests that women have a 'cold perverted will' (55) because they are as fickle and as cold as the wind. The physical chill of the wind seems to convey the sadness Clare feels at Mary's remoteness from him.

CHECK THE POEM
More May Day activities are featured in Clare's poem 'Sport in the Meadows'.

GLOSSARY

1	**pewit**	peewit, lapwing or plover
39	**owns**	recognises as familiar, or acknowledges as having power over oneself

---

AN INVITE TO ETERNITY

- The poet asks a maiden whether she is prepared to share his life, even though it is dark and nightmarish.

Using repetitive and therefore insistent questioning, the poet invites a woman to share his life, even though it is one of deep **melancholy**. He asks if she will accompany him on his journey through his difficult life. The landscape of this metaphorical journey is nightmarish and dangerous, and he suggests that the journey is also like his own lack of identity. The land he will take her to is a land of shadows, where they will not even be able to recognise each other's faces. If the woman can accept all of this, then they should be together for ever.

CHECK THE BOOK
The journey, seen as a metaphor for life, is the main **trope** of John Bunyan's *The Pilgrim's Progress* (1678–84). See also Clare's 'Love and Memory'.

COMMENTARY

Melancholy is characterised in a number of ways in this poem. It is seen in biblical terms, through the reference to the valley of the shadow of death; in psychological terms, through the references to the loss of identity; and in terms of the natural world, through the references to the extremes of nature.

The invitation extended by the poet is an invitation to marriage: to spend a whole life together and, beyond that, to spend eternity together. This arrangement, however, is not presented attractively. It offers an honest, soul-bearing vision of what life with the poet will be like: dark. This darkness stands for melancholy or depression: there is no visible path, because depression cannot be navigated easily; there is no light, because there is no hope for the end of depression; there is no life, because depression is like death.

The poet will take the maiden to a place where a flood will cover the stones at the bottom of a stream. The flood is a destructive image that suggests the poet's identity will be overwhelmed with sadness. He describes the flood in a curious way: the stones will turn from neutral things into the flood itself, rather than being covered by it. Through this image Clare describes the negation of self that he experiences in depression. A similar image of flooding follows this in the **simile** 'plains will rise like ocean waves' (10); Clare repeats the curious metamorphic image that he has used in the previous line: the plains turn *into* ocean waves. 'And mountains darken into caves' (12) is also metamorphic and suggests that something tall and magnificent will become dark and subterranean. This will be a place where life is as intangible as a dream.

Having described the landscape up to this point, the poet now talks in similar terms about the landscape of personality. The physical landscape has, nevertheless, prior to this been a **metaphor** for personality. Here, however, he talks about the breakdown of his personality by talking about the breakdown of his familial and social relationships. He is also, perhaps, referring to the loss of memory. Without memory there is no personal identity; he will live, in the future, without the things that constitute his own identity: his life, his home and his name. He will lose all of these, and merely exist. Although he references Shakespeare's famous **soliloquy** spoken by Hamlet about avenging his father's death ('To be, or not to be', *Hamlet*, III.1.56–68), Clare means merely to draw attention to the fact that he will exist in the future without retaining his current identity: 'At once to be, and not to be' (21). Hamlet uses these words to convey a different point: to talk about whether he is going to act or not, and possibly to die or commit suicide as a consequence. Clare's line 'That was, and is not' (22) also refers to the poet's loss of identity in the future, when the world will seem as though it is made from shadows. Here Clare is possibly referring to Plato's cave (see also the reference to caves in line 12). Shadows have no identity; they are not physical forms. The final part of the penultimate **stanza** suggests that the couple will be surrounded by sky, as if in the heavens.

In the final stanza, the poet continues the idea of the future being a 'land of shadows' (25) in which his identity will be lost. He says that they will not be able to recognise each other, and it will be a life where time is confused, because identity is confused. The word 'trace' (25) means 'walk' in this context, but it also suggests that the journey will be repeated, as in to trace over something. The idea of retracing footsteps comes again in the second part of the stanza, where Clare suggests that the maiden will follow in his footsteps if she agrees to join her life with his. The last line is the most explicit reference to the poem being about a marriage. This is more than marriage in the Christian sense, however. According to the Anglican marriage ceremony, husbands and wives are separated at death ('till death do us part'). The poet implies a longer union that will last through the afterlife. The marriage will not be happy, however. He talks of the union as joining 'the living with the dead' (30): the maiden represents life; the depressed poet represents death. Clare describes in this poem a world of reversals, where good things are turned into their counterparts.

GLOSSARY

25	trace	walk

CHECK THE POEM

The poem is dated 1848 and is written in Clare's favourite **couplets**. It is **thematically** similar to 'I Am'. Both poems are quite complex at a **syntactical** level. In 'An Invite to Eternity', for example, the lines 'the path hath lost its way' (5) and 'the sun forgets the day' (6) in the second part of the first stanza suggest the **personification** of the inanimate path and sun, but give the effect of the poet having lost his way.

CONTEXT

Plato's *Republic* (Book 7) uses the **allegory** of the cave as a way of describing the difficulty of knowing the real world. The untutored are chained in a cave with their backs to the light, facing a wall. They see only shadows on a wall and mistake this for reality. Only those who have escaped from the cave are fit to rule.

LOVE AND MEMORY

- The poet's lover has died young and he mourns her loss.
- He is not consoled by his knowledge that she is in heaven and is happy.
- Some consolation is found in the cycles of the natural world, but he cannot imagine an end to his grief.

CONTEXT

Hades is often used as the equivalent of Hell but it is merely the place where the dead were thought to go, and the Greek name for the god who ruled over this region.

CONTEXT

In Greek mythology the Fates were three goddesses who controlled birth, life and death by a mystical thread. Clotho (Greek for 'to draw thread') presided over birth by using the distaff (a long pole on which the fibres for the thread were spun); Lachesis (Greek for 'destiny') spun the thread and determined the length of the thread and therefore the life; Atropos (Greek for 'unchangeable') severed the thread of life with scissors.

The poet mourns his dead lover, and thinks back to the happy times they spent together. She was beautiful and dear to him, but now she is in heaven. He tries to console himself, but finds no pleasure in life without her. All things die, as the cycles of the year show, and there is some consolation in that, but there is also great sadness in her loss. Her death has taken his very essence away, and he cannot put his grief into words.

COMMENTARY

The poet addresses his dead lover, opening with a formal statement about the finality of death and the futility of mourning. Although described as 'fruitless' (3), mourning is inevitable for him because he dwells on the happy life they had together. Her death is likened to a dark journey away from the poet, and there is no hope of return. Clare may be **alluding** to the classical underworld, Hades, reached by crossing the mythical river, Styx. He mixes his **metaphors** in order to give a sense of the liveliness, beauty, happiness and richness of their life together. Laughter is a sound, but it is seen on the forehead of the dead woman. This laughter is, furthermore, a metaphor for their life together, and her death has caused desolation for the poet.

In their youth, it seemed to him that they would live for ever, because youth seemed to embrace her with a 'halo' (11). This religious **symbol** suggests that she was a heavenly presence on earth. When she was alive, there was an essence of immortality about her; she was saintly. Clare draws on pagan and Christian traditions in the word 'weave' (10), associated with the Fates of classical mythology. It also suggests a humble activity: making cloth. A woven halo may even suggest the Passion of Christ: thorns were woven into a crown and placed on his head during the Crucifixion. Believing that the woman is immortal is, however, an earthly deception. The poet uses three superlatives to describe his love: 'fairest', 'dearest' (13) and 'nearest' (15). Of all of the women he found beautiful, she was the most beautiful, the one he loved most, and the one who was closest to him. However, the final line of the second **stanza** is a little puzzling, in that one would expect the poet to refer to the name of the woman at this point. He says, however, that 'this name' (16) is in his heart, and not 'thy name'. In other versions of the poem 'thy' is used, and we can, perhaps, make a case for Clare meaning to refer to the woman at this point.

In the third stanza the poet uses a natural metaphor that picks up on the previous reference to the woman being the 'nearest' to him. The closer the stream is to the source – or 'fountain' (17) – the purer the water is; the rosebud is 'sweeter' (19) to the imagination than a fully blossomed rose. These two images of immaturity (the spring and the rosebud) suggest purity and love, and describe the poet's feelings about the woman now that she is dead: his thoughts about her are purer than anything on earth.

The next stanza makes it clearer that the woman was young when she died, her beauty short-lived because she died too soon. She is like the green bud in spring because she died young and, like the blossomed rose, her beauty has reached its height. Her beauty was such that when she arrived in heaven, she was too beautiful to be merely human. Clare perhaps alludes at this point to the myth of Prometheus when he calls humankind 'earth's tenants of clay' (30). He may also be referring to the Book of Job in the Old Testament: 'I also am formed out of the clay' (Job 33:6) and 'Remember, I beseech thee, that thou hast made me as the clay' (Job 10:9).

The poet questions why he is grieving, given that he knows she must be happy in heaven. Nevertheless, it is because she has gone that he feels her loss so deeply. Her presence 'possessed' all that he loved and enjoyed, and her absence has 'destroyed' all that he loved and enjoyed. The objects of the two verbs 'possessed' (37) and 'destroyed' (38) are in the final two lines of the stanza. His conclusion is that her life was more precious than his own, and so intertwined with his sense of self, that he feels as if he has died too: 'My being is gone' (84). The poem is dated 1828.

> **CONTEXT**
>
> According to Apollodorus, the Titan Prometheus made the first man and woman out of clay, bringing them to life with fire that he had stolen from heaven.

> **CONTEXT**
>
> Clare paraphrased Job 38–41 in verse in the late 1830s and early 1840s.

> **? QUESTION**
>
> Do you think Clare idealises the woman in this poem? Is this another poem about Mary Joyce?

QUESTION

Look at the two other poems in this section of the Everyman collection, 'Song: "The morning mist is changing blue"' and 'Ballad: "I dreamt not what it was to woo"'. How do they compare?

GLOSSARY

17	**fountain**	spring or source of water issuing from the earth
26	**blown**	blossomed
59	**blea**	bleak, wild

LOSS AND THE POLITICS OF NATURE

REMEMBRANCES

- The poet compares and contrasts past happiness with present sorrow.
- He is particularly struck by how unexpected this sorrow is and how devastating enclosure has been for the local landscape.

Clare looks back over the year and laments the passing of summer. He tries to call to mind the pleasures of that season, but cannot. He had thought that this joy would always remain with him, but now there is only silence. He describes childhood activities, and reveals that he never dreamed that such pleasures would fade. If he had known then what he knows now, he would have stayed awake for the whole of his childhood in order to maximise his experience.

COMMENTARY

'Remembrances' (1832) laments the passing of the summer and, with it, the pleasures and exuberance of the natural world. As the names of the places and the experiences all belong to Clare, it is worth speculating that this is a particularly personal **elegy** to the passing of Clare's childhood. Now that this season has passed, Clare explains what the summer once meant to him and what he associates it with, namely happiness, joy, energy and activity. The summer also stands for his early life. He uses energetic images of change, activity, noise and movement to convey the vitality and flux that summer causes; in contrast, the bleak reality of autumn and winter is expressed in static, harsh and barren images, like the 'stone' (8), the 'silence' (9), the 'chill' (43), the 'desert' (48), and the 'battle-strife' (60).

CONTEXT

Eric Robinson and David Powell note, in their glossary of John Clare's *Major Works*, that '"clink" may be onomatopoeic, expressive of the contact of marble; alternatively, it may signify "clench", in which case "clink and bandy chock" may denote marbles played by first "clenching" the thumb and then allowing it, on release, to strike the marble as the bandy or hockey-stick strikes the ball' (1984, pp. 508–9).

LOSS AND THE POLITICS OF NATURE

The representations of Clare's past experiences of summer all involve a close engagement with the natural world: lying down and singing on the bank of the spring, tying willow branches to make a swing, fishing, making a cart to transport the harvest and cutting straw. All of these activities are seen as pleasurable, but each set of summer visions is broken by the intrusion of the colder seasons causing the heart to become heavy, and introducing the idea of the sorrow of parting, and the sting of pain. Clare also chooses natural images to put across the seasonal threat to the summer idyll by comparing it to a flock of birds which fly south to a warmer climate, leaving behind an empty landscape.

The first part of the fourth **stanza** talks of childhood memories which anticipate manhood, focusing on the poet as a boy copying the gait of a grown man and pretending to do the work of an adult by ploughing with a 'willow twig' (33). The second section begins after the **caesura** and returns to the present, voicing an emotional reaction to such recollections. After the memory of the places of his childhood appears in the poet's mind, it leaves behind a feeling of **melancholy**, which is indicated by the emitting of a sigh. Continuing in the present tense, the poet describes what he now sees in this natural landscape, namely the 'little mouldiwarps hang sweeing to the wind / On the only aged willow' (37–8). Nature is **personified** as a viewer of this natural scene and her reaction echoes the mood of the poet, for she 'hides her face' (39) at the sight of the single and forlorn willow tree, and laments in a 'silent murmuring' (40).

Clare continues the lament for the absence of visual contact with the delights that summer brings in stanza five, and notes the changes in the landscape which have occurred over time and as a result of the start of the colder seasons. The commons or uncultivated meadows have disappeared, and the moles – 'little homeless miners' (43) – are now threatened by traps. The details of rural life that he now misses indicate that he appreciates the aesthetic beauty of the natural landscape and possesses a **sensibility** which gives attention to the 'daisy gemmed in dew' (45) and the 'hills of silken grass like to cushions to the view' (46). Again the winter **imagery** concludes the stanza, as the poet persists in explaining that the summer landscape has been stripped of its beauty, 'levelled like a desert' (48) and 'vanished like the sun' (49). This idea is continued in the sixth

 CHECK THE NET
Visit the John Clare Page at **www.johnclare.info** – this is an informative site with a number of interesting articles and essays, extensive indexes to Clare's works, and links to other useful sites on Clare and the Romantic period. John Goodridge has also compiled an extensive critical bibliography which can be found on this website.

Napoleon
(1769–1821) rose
to prominence
during the French
Revolution,
eventually
becoming emperor
in 1804. After
pursuing several
military campaigns
in Europe, he
installed members
of his family on
the thrones of
Spain, Italy,
Westphalia and
Naples, and
overcame the
governments
of the Swiss
Confederation, the
Confederation of
the Rhine and the
Duchy of Warsaw.
His marriage to
Marie-Louise,
daughter of
Francis I of Austria,
also put Austria in
his power.

**CHECK
THE NET**

The Napoleon
Foundation
supports an
extensive website
dedicated to the
former emperor and
his family: visit
www.napoleon.org

stanza, where the bare fields, overcast skies and the destruction of 'boyhood's pleasing haunts' (57) where he used to play are attributed to the evil-doings of winter. Winter has the power to 'petrify' (54), shrivel, wither and trample down (58), words which do not suggest hope of renewal or rebirth after the season has passed, but instead promote the idea of finality.

Clare views the desolation in the landscape from the standpoint of an observer of the natural scene in the present. Winter has not only changed the countryside physically into a bleak and cold scene, it has also altered the places of his childhood almost beyond recognition. This idea of displacement and alienation from places of memory is coupled here with the image of enclosure. Clare likens the act of enclosure to the military ambitions and tactics of Napoleon Bonaparte, and ultimately to the effects of winter: 'It levelled every bush and tree and levelled every hill / And hung the moles for traitors' (68–9). The poet is now cut off from past joys, and the moles that lived in freedom on the commons have been killed, brutally strung up like political opponents.

The final stanza returns to the emotional landscape of the poet – to joy and love, which are so closely connected to the enjoyment of the land. With hindsight, and now situated in the impoverished rural location of the present, the poet says he would have cherished these emotions more, had he been more vigilant. He would have prevented nature, here **personified** as a lover, from leaving him, and would have wooed her once again.

'Remembrances' is not merely a seasonal song that expresses delight in the summer; it contains the protests of a distressed and dejected poet against the destruction of his personal identity, which is located in this now changed rural setting. Unable to protect the flora and fauna of this environment, he not only experiences an expulsion from this Eden but also the loss of the emotions associated with this place. Even Clare's poetic testimony to the lost days is portrayed as a poor substitute for the real thing: 'O words are poor receipts for what time hath stole away' (29).

GLOSSARY

8	**'chock'** a game played by tossing marbles into a hole. To chock is to throw
	'taw' a marble
22	**haws** red fruit of hawthorn
37	**mouldiwarps** moles
39	**sweeing** swinging
47	**pismire** ant

DECAY, A BALLAD

- The poet realises that his creative imagination is on the decline.
- He remembers the natural settings which used to be the inspiration for his poetry.

The poet laments that his poetry is drying up along with his imaginative life. It seems as if nature, who inspires the poet, has moved house. Clare talks of the aspects of the natural world that attracted him: these were simple and ordinary sights. He links the idea of the loss of creativity with close reference to the natural world, implying that the loss of the poetic vision is akin to the loss of paradise.

COMMENTARY

'Decay, a Ballad' (1832) links **thematically** with 'Remembrances' and 'The Flitting', which focus on the loss of the natural landscape and the creative and emotional implications of this for the nature poet. The opening line, 'O poesy is on the wane', or a variant of it, is repeated in each of the **refrains** of the **ballad** and introduces the subject of the loss of creativity. The refrain counterbalances the stanza so that the first part of each stanza is positive, and the last part is negative.

The poet laments that the images that enter his mind are not suitable representations of the subject matter, and consequently his ability to write poetry is quickly fading. Nature, the focus of his writing,

CHECK THE POEM

The **conceit** of a poet writing about not being able to write is used by Keats in 'Ode to a Nightingale' (written in 1819). Here the poet laments that he cannot write verse which is as accomplished as the music of the bird, and he searches for inspiration, producing a poem while he does so. Wordsworth's *The Prelude* (published in 1850) searches for a topic for an epic, and turns into an epic.

CONTEXT

Wordsworth and Coleridge admired and wrote simple poems. Their *Lyrical Ballads* (1798) moved away from a more ornate eighteenth-century style of poetry to an accessible, almost prosaic, verse style.

CONTEXT

The laurel wreath was given by the Greeks to the winner in the Pythian Games, and is associated with poetry and prophecy.

(**personified**), appears to be 'on the flitting' (4), as if she is leaving him to go somewhere else. All of the aspects of the natural world that represent her, the fields, grass and beautiful places, 'Are sighing "Going, all a-going"' (8). In the second **stanza** the poet declares that he valued the wild, natural phenomena such as 'The bank with brambles overspread / And little molehills' (11–12) more than the laurel tree, a **symbol** of poetic distinction. The finely designed paths and cut grass that one would find in cultivated gardens are devoid of the richness that he found in the uneven surfaces of 'rutty lanes' (17) and in the heaths (18). Thinking about his relationship with nature, the poet recalls sitting by 'pasture streams' (21) when nature's beauty was comparable with the Garden of Eden. It was also a landscape that reminded him of love. Clare hints at personification again when he says he 'sat with love' (21) and 'beauty's self' (22), but these references can also be seen as **alluding** to a love that he perceived to be in the landscape. The central image in this third stanza is of drinking, even when not thirsty, in order to toast love. Christ's miracle of turning water into wine (John 2: 1–11), called here 'nectar from the sky' (27), is also referred to: love is able to turn 'water into wine' (28).

Still picturing how things once were, the poet remembers the morning sun when the clouds were like foreign mountains (31–2) and the heavens engaged in the act of looking upon his mind. The experience of this remembered beauty is cut short, however, by the realisation that 'These heavens are gone, the mountains grey / Turned mist' (35–6); this statement is marked by a **caesura** that introduces the present tense, and a description of the current state of the natural landscape. Clare uses the image of the estranged sun which has lost its way in 'The Flitting' too (55–6). In 'Decay, a Ballad' there is a supplementary emphasis on the sun wandering like a 'homeless ranger' (36). The nomadic sun does not disappear; it pursues its 'naked way / Unnoticed like a very stranger' (37–8).

At the end of stanza four a change occurs in the second line of the **refrain**, from 'I hardly know her face again' and 'I cannot find her face again' to 'Nor love nor joy is mine again' (40). This indicates that the poet is reflecting now on the changes in his emotions. His happiness at watching the beauty of this **metaphorical** sunset is such that he is driven to grief by it. It is as if the sun will never return: 'I often think that west is gone' (43). The sunset inaugurates a 'cruel time' of dark reality (44). The **elegiac** lines 'The sky hangs o'er a broken dream, / The brambles dwindled to a bramble' (47–8) characterise a natural landscape that is weakening and decaying. Connected to this image is the poet's realisation that his own imaginative powers and creative expression are diminishing: 'Mere withered stalks and fading trees / And pastures spread with hills and rushes / Are all my fading vision sees' (51–3). Clare observes that because his poetic vision is leaving him, his emotional experience of the natural world has changed. He can see a wasteland in place of what was formerly a magical setting, where mushrooms used to resemble 'fairy bowers' (55).

The mood is heightened in the following stanza, where poetry is mentioned at the beginning rather than the end. Instead of being on the decline, it has finally 'passed away' (61) like the coming of night. The action of 'undeceiving', used in lines 44 and 62, suggests that his imagination, or fancy, has lost the artistic skill to perform the act of deception. The poet attempts to console himself with the knowledge that he has experienced paradise and love, and should be grateful, but the inevitable refrain reminds us that the misery caused by the decay of the poetic vision will not be relieved.

Gradual departure, a feature of much of the poem, is described next in the context of friendship. The cooling of his friends has been like the cooling of embers in the fire. Acts of pretending, play-acting and jesting dominate the final stanza, but they are also images of trickery and deception. The foolishness of April Fool's Day reminds him of the inventiveness and deception that he has enjoyed through his poetic imagination. Hope is singled out as being something that plays at deceiving, whereas joy is 'the art of true believing' (78): it can only be experienced when one has no doubts. The final thought in the last refrain repeats the **tragic** sense of his fading poetic skill; the poet longs to believe it will return. It is **ironic**, however, that in the act of lamenting the loss of his poetry, Clare has indeed produced a poem.

CONTEXT

'April day' (73) – April Fool's Day, or All Fools' Day (1 April) – has been celebrated in Britain since the mid seventeenth century. Steve Roud notes, in *The English Year* (2006), that it 'probably came from France or Germany' (p. 94). It was usual to send people on pointless errands: 'Pigeon's milk, hen's teeth, and a book about Eve's mother are other traditional items that fools were regularly sent to find. The simpler tricks, such as gluing a coin to the floor … seem to have been a later development, perhaps from the mid nineteenth century onwards' (p. 96).

GLOSSARY

4	**flitting** to move house

CHECK THE BOOK

Mark Storey calls this poem 'a mixture of sustained lyricism and half-mad invective' (*The Poetry of John Clare: A Critical Introduction*, 1974, p. 195).

CONTEXT

Clare uses the simplicity of the **ballad stanza** (four lines rhyming *abab*) to powerful effect in this poem. Its simplicity and apocalyptic **tone** recall the poetry of the Romantic poet, artist and illustrator William Blake (1757–1827).

CHECK THE NET

Blake's poetry and art reflect his apocalyptic visions. To see some of Blake's writing and images, visit the William Blake Archive at **www.blakearchive. org**

SONG: LAST DAY

- The poet has a vision of the Apocalypse.
- Clare gives the Apocalypse a personal gloss when he talks about it as his own vision.

The poem begins with a statement of surety that the Apocalypse will one day happen. Basing his **imagery** on biblical accounts, the poet describes the various horrific events that will be seen on the last day of the world. The destruction of the heavens and earth, and the onset of oblivion are conjured up in a hellish scene of death. Those who have sinned will go to hell; the poet wonders whether this will include him. The poem ends with the poet considering, again, the nature of the Apocalypse. He is certain that at the Apocalypse he will be remembered.

COMMENTARY

Written in 1845, this is one of Clare's late poems, and it dates to the time when he was a patient at Northampton General Lunatic Asylum. It therefore makes sense to treat this poem autobiographically.

The poem opens with an apocalyptic statement announcing the certainty that the last day will come. The phrase 'Still following the past' (2) is a concise way of signalling that the events are in the future and are inevitable; this 'dreadful day' (1) is the Apocalypse. On this day, according to Christian tradition, the sun and moon will disappear, and will 'mingle with the blast' (4). This 'blast' may be the roar of the sea or wind, or the sound of the last trumpet. The last trumpet is a reference to I Corinthians 15:52: 'In a moment, in the twinkling of an eye, at the last trump: for the trumpet shall sound, and the dead shall be raised incorruptible, and we shall be changed.'

Clare next describes how real his vision of the Apocalypse seems: 'There is a vision in my eye' (5). The poet reveals that his mind feels as if it is empty, a 'vacuum' (6), and it is as if he is lying on the sea in the middle of a storm. Clare frequently uses the storm image to signify emotional upset, and so it is likely here that he is referring to his psychological trauma. We can see this in 'I Am', where he talks of being 'like vapours tossed' (6) 'Into the living sea of waking dreams' (8), and his life being like a 'shipwreck' (10). The same can be said of 'Song: "A seaboy on the giddy mast"', in which the poet feels 'o'erwhelmed' (11) by the storm, and his life is likened to 'the ocean storm, / A black and troubled sea' (13–14).

The second stanza continues the imagery from the Book of Revelation. Valleys will turn into mountainous waves and 'mountains sink to seas' (10), reversing the peaks and troughs of the natural world. It will be a time when towns, cities, churches and graveyards will disappear. Clare uses a natural **simile** here: they will 'vanish like a breeze' (12); the unnatural will take on the attributes of the natural. In anticipating that days will no longer mark the passing of time, the sky is likened to an 'almanac' (14), because both keep track of time. Oblivion, an important word used often when Clare talks about memory and fame, is **personified** in this stanza. The 'shades' (17) and 'shadows' (19) that he often associates with being forgotten are also **alluded** to at this point. We are told that oblivion, the state of forgetting, will destroy everything (13–16): in other words, history will be forgotten. The repetition of 'pays', at the end of line 16 and the beginning of line 17, gives weight to the seriousness of the vision; 'hell' is placed at the end of line 17 for emphasis.

Using language predominantly connected with darkness and destruction in the third stanza, Clare introduces the idea of heaven and hell into this apocalyptic vision. Hell is depicted here as a dark place in the depths where 'sulphur's shadows dwell' (19). 'Sin' here stands for all those who have sinned; Clare's point is that sinners will go to hell when the world ends. 'Worth' stands for those who are worthy to be saved; these will go to heaven, in other words wear 'the crown' (20). Here Clare draws attention, again, to his sight, reminding us that this is a mystical vision. He uses an unusual image of a shore that has 'shrivelled to a scroll' (22). This may be a simple image of dryness; it may have a literary **connotation**; or it may have a link with Revelation 6:14: 'And the heaven departed as a scroll when it is rolled together; and every mountain and island were moved out of their places.' The stanza ends with the suggestion that the heavens are being pulled away from the poet, and he can hear thunder and smell sulphur. The

> **CONTEXT**
>
> Clare employs a number of images from the Book of Revelation: 'the sun became black as sackcloth of hair, and the moon became as blood' (6:12); 'And the second angel sounded, and as it were a great mountain burning with fire was cast into the sea: and the third part of the sea became blood' (8:8).

> **CONTEXT**
>
> Isaiah 34:4 also uses an image of a scroll when commenting on the power of God to destroy: 'And all the host of heaven shall be dissolved, and the heavens shall be rolled together as a scroll: and all their host shall fall down, as the leaf falleth off from the vine, and as a falling fig from the fig tree.'

CONTEXT

Thunder is mentioned throughout the Book of Revelation and signifies the action of God and the violence of the end of the world. Revelation 6:13 states: 'And the stars of heaven fell unto the earth, even as a fig tree casteth her untimely figs, when she is shaken of a mighty wind.' In Revelation 21 John sees a vision of the New Jerusalem 'coming down from God out of heaven' (21:2).

 CHECK THE POEM

In 1841 Clare paraphrased, in verse, Revelation 21 ('The New Jerusalem Rev. Chap 21st') and Revelation 22 ('The River of the Water of Life – Rev. Chap. 22').

change in tense puts the action into the present for immediacy, even though he is describing a future event.

In the final **stanza** the stars are described as turning to 'dun' (26). Heaven is bent over by this darkness – 'bowed' (27) – and is seen as putting an end to the day's light when the stars and skies 'decay' (29). The destruction of heaven at the Apocalypse refers to Revelation 21:1: 'And I saw a new heaven and a new earth: for the first heaven and the first earth were passed away; and there was no more sea.'

The final line of the poem addresses an unidentified person. The poet says that when the Apocalypse comes, he will be remembered by someone. This line is enigmatic, but it may refer to the good thief's words to Jesus, who was crucified next to him. The thief repents and says to Christ: 'Lord, remember me when thou comest into thy kingdom' (Luke 23:42). Jesus's reply is: 'Verily I say unto thee, To day shalt thou be with me in paradise' (23:43). Clare is possibly asking to be remembered by Christ: being remembered, as the thief's words show, constitutes a request that Clare be counted among those who are saved. We could read this line in terms of Clare's personal life; he may be informing the reader that he will be remembered by the person who is or was the most important in his life. Perhaps, given Clare's preoccupation with lasting fame, the poet is also telling his readers that we will remember him.

GLOSSARY

14	**almanac**	calendar
23	**rend**	pull violently or tear
26	**dun**	dark
32	**thou'lt**	thou wilt, you will

THE LAMENT OF SWORDY WELL

- Swordy Well, the imagined persona of an ancient stone quarry, feels defenceless against those who exploit the land and the poor for financial gain.
- It speaks out against social injustice, oppression, enclosure and the destruction of the countryside and the livelihood of the rural community.

The poem describes how petitioners may seem pious, but if they do not receive what they want they become angry and curse. They are, however, no worse than people who go to church and ask God for things. The voice of the poem, which is the quarry in the title, tells us of the suffering and enslavement it has endured since the parish has owned it. The quarry wishes to be returned to its original state.

COMMENTARY

'The Lament of Swordy Well' (1821–4) is a **ballad** about the enclosure of a beautiful old stone quarry near to where Clare lived. It is, like 'The Nightingale's Nest' and 'The Lamentations of Round-Oak Waters', a **dramatic monologue**: 'I'm Swordy Well, a piece of land' (21). The landscape voices its sense of loss directly using **colloquial** and **idiomatic** English. A close connection is made between the treatment of the land and the suffering of the people who work on it. The fates of the farmers and the landscape are identical, for both have fallen into the hands of the parish, which exploits them for profit. The quarry has been given to the overseers in the parish in order to provide stone for mending the roads. This means that the natural habitat of the quarry, which Clare enjoyed for its butterflies, lizards and wild flowers, has been destroyed.

The poem opens with a statement which unmasks the 'Petitioners': they may seem full of good intentions, but they are corrupt and grasping. In comparison, the quarry has no possessions, not even a hat to beg with (9–10), or a physical impairment that a beggar would use to earn a living. The targets of its criticism are 'profit' (13) and 'Gain' (15), financial goals **personified** as male figures performing the lowly acts of getting their 'clutches' (13) in and 'stooping' to pick up even 'a single pin' (15) from the floor for their own advantage (13–16). The action of pinning something to one's sleeve may refer to the medieval chivalric custom where a knight pinned to his sleeve a token – a pledge of loyalty – given to him by the lady he admired. As there is no token here, there is no loyalty. Pins were quite cheap to buy, so the reference may also mean that 'Gain' is so careful not to miss an opportunity that he will pick up something that is relatively worthless. This may also be a good luck ritual. The rhyme 'See a pin and pick it up, / All the day you'll have good luck' was first recorded in 1842, but it is possible that this is an earlier **allusion** to it. The quarry uses a double negative – 'I never

CHECK THE BOOK

John Barrell writes in *The Idea of Landscape and the Sense of Place 1730–1840: An Approach to the Poetry of John Clare* (1972) that 'Clare's writing after 1821 or so is increasingly preoccupied with being "local"' (p. 120). For a longer quotation and further discussion see **Themes: Village life**.

pin / No troubles to my breast' (17–18) – in order to give the impression of **colloquial** speech. That it does not wear its troubles on its breast means it is not open about its suffering.

Gain, profit, pity, trouble, cunning, want, dependence and loss feature in this poem almost as characters; their **personification** enables their attributes to interact more dramatically with the life of the quarry. An elaborate **metaphor** compares the quarry's harsh life with earning a living by farming. This is particularly resonant for Clare's own life as an agricultural worker, as he found it hard to earn a living by it. The bountiful harvest, also personified, 'Leaves losses' taunts' (30) with the quarry, and 'gain comes yearly with the plough' (31) to force it to continue the work. Later in the poem 'gain' emerges as the main incentive which motivates the oppressors, causing the loss of freedom (141) and the enclosure of the land in pounds or pens (151). The quarry was not a suitable place for farming, so this is not a literal description of land being used in this way. It is more likely to be a way of describing, **figuratively**, the drudgery and unfairness of life as an agricultural worker in order to heighten the awareness of the quarry's overwork and ruin. The enslavement of the worker is also seen in **stanza** five, which focuses on dependence. Dependence is personified as 'a brute' (33).

Although personified, Swordy Well recognises that it is not human: 'I'm no man' (41). It nevertheless wants to follow noble causes, seek justice and express its protest in a song, in other words the **ballad** (41–4). Focusing on the past, it reminisces about when the price of grain rose during the Napoleonic Wars and it 'trembled with alarms' (50), and when the prices fell again and it was saved. Notably, the effects of war are seen as doing less damage to this environment than those who enforce the Act of Enclosure (see **Historical background**).

The town's possession of Swordy Well has led to the physical deterioration of the land: 'The silver springs, grown naked dykes, / Scarce own a bunch of rushes' (57–8). It has now become bare, naked and barren. Its 'trees, banks and bushes' (60) have been dug up, the soil tilled, and the 'sand and grit and stones' (62) removed so that it is now a skeleton (60–64 and 105–8). The once proud Swordy Well declares that its stone built the town, and it used to 'keep' or sustain 'horses, cows and sheep' (69) but never owned them, for the

---

CONTEXT

Britain was at war with France between February 1793 and March 1802, when there was a short peace, known as the Peace of Amiens, and then fighting resumed in May 1803, continuing until the defeat of Napoleon in 1815. The harvests of 1794, 1795, 1799 and 1800 were particularly poor, and Britain was forced to import its grain. The price of grain rose because of the shortage, and there were food riots and political demonstrations.

ownership of a living thing involves enslaving it. It compares its sophistication and age with the people who live near it: it was looking after livestock when they barely had domestic animals, and is far more ancient than they are: 'These things that claim my own as theirs / Were born but yesterday' (65–6). Later the enclosed landscape declares that it does not claim ownership over any part of itself: 'I've scarce a nook to call my own' (113).

In contrast to Swordy Well, the parish does not have an interest in 'keeping' or supporting life on its land. The quarry argues that the parish would even let the bees die 'To save an extra keep' (76). The equivalent human **tragedy** of the plight of the bees is the starvation and poverty seen in the workhouse (79–80). Pride has a workhouse, and it takes away whatever the poor can produce; the quarry is also a workhouse, but, conversely, it protects its fields.

By letting the land speak in place of the field labourer, Clare closely intertwines the issue of social injustice with the subject of the exploitation of the natural landscape. Disenfranchised and dispossessed, Swordy Well does not 'whine and beg' (121) or hang 'lies on pity's peg / To bring a grist to mill' (123–4); instead it describes the reality of being stripped of all of its natural assets which fall into the hands of the greedy: 'My only tree they've left a stump / And nought remains my own' (127–8). To reinforce the idea of human destitution, Clare uses the image of stripping the natural landscape in combination with ideas of nakedness and wearing rags. He does this by creating images which relate to both the human and the natural world: for example the greedy are described as tearing 'The very grass from off my back' (139), and Swordy Well's freedom is a 'dull suit' (142) that it no longer wears. If the price of grain increases further, through shortage, then the land will be in demand, so it asks God to 'send the grain to fall' (166) to ensure the land's protection.

Swordy Well speaks in defence of the poor and identifies with them because they used to come for miles to see its landscape and appreciate its beauty (153–6); now they pass by and sigh in sympathy for its plight (158–60). Feeling forsaken, Swordy Well calls upon God to reward it for its former benevolence and philanthropy towards the poor, who always found shelter there (169–76). As a common space, Swordy Well was once able to

CHECK THE POEM

Clare's poem 'The Workhouse Orphan, A Tale' (1821) is worth looking at in this context.

CONTEXT

The workhouse became part of a national system after the 1834 Poor Law Amendment Act, though workhouses had existed independently before that time. The rules that governed every aspect of life there made them like prisons. Men, women and children were separated; the diet was poor; and the regime was such that only the desperate would go there. Work of a dull and repetitive nature, such as stone-breaking, was exchanged for room and board. Workhouses were abolished in 1930.

CONTEXT

'Grist to the mill' is something useful or profitable. Grist is the quantity of grain ground at one time.

support the peasants and guarantee their freedom. The private cultivation of the land and its 'vile enclosure' (183) has led directly to the enslavement of the rural workers: 'There was a time my bit of ground / Made freemen of the slave' (177). In contrast to the rural peasants, the gypsies are viewed here as being outside of regular social structures, and free from such economic processes and constraints, for they are able to move away (181–6). Like Clare, they reject boundaries: 'No parish bounds they like' (186). Comparing itself to the gypsies, the quarry declares that if it were left alone it would not break the law, or rebel in any way. It also makes an interesting association, linking Christians with Turks. This means that it thinks that Turks are savages.

The final two **stanzas** contain Swordy Well's wishes for the future: to be used for sheep farming and to be left unploughed (193–200). Enclosure will alter the 'face' (204) of the land, but it longs to be rejuvenated by the spring, and sees itself as the last of the fields. Swordy Well's undoing will be the quarry, however, and the 'stone pits' and 'delving holes' (205) it provides and which are profitable to people. Its final thought is that all that will remain of it is its name.

CONTEXT

Clare is likely to have absorbed his view of the Turks from Byron's so-called 'Turkish Tales'. In the six tales grouped together under this heading, including *The Bride of Abydos* (1813) and *The Corsair* (1814), Turkish men are portrayed as 'a male ideal of the commanding type that proves itself in war and government' (Mohammed Sharafuddin, *Islam and Romantic Orientalism: Literary Encounters with the Orient*, 1994, p. 249).

GLOSSARY

3	**forbears** withholds
26	**shift** gaining a living in any fashion, including fraud
59	**tykes** lazy or ill-mannered men from the lower classes
89	**clover bottle** bunch of clover
100	**dyke** a hollow dugout that holds water
112	**tussocks** tufts of coarse grass
117	**Stock** livestock
123	**hing** hang
161	**clack** gossip
164	**fain** glad
165	**lorn** forlorn
179	**pindar'd** a pindar is someone employed to impound stray cattle

JOHN CLARE, POET

'I AM'

- In this short and powerful poem the poet contemplates personal identity and loneliness, and yet, paradoxically, a need to be alone.
- He longs for the peace he found in childhood, and to be at one with God.

Clare describes how he feels abandoned by his friends, and how, in his mental turmoil, even those he loves the best seem like strangers to him. He longs for a peaceful place where he can be undisturbed by others, and be at one with his 'Creator' (15).

COMMENTARY

Composed in 1846, and published for the first time in the *Bedford Times* on 1 January 1848, 'I Am' is one of Clare's most famous poems. Clare wrote this poem at about the same time as 'Sonnet: "I Am"', which has a similar **theme**. The poem is concerned with identity, and as such has much in common with 'An Invite to Eternity' (printed later in the same month in the *Bedford Times* on 29 January 1848). All three poems deal with mental anguish and the despair accompanied by fear of insanity.

The poem begins with the emphatic statement 'I am'. Here the poet baldly states that he exists. This declaration is qualified after a pause, indicated by a dash, and we are given a more emotional gloss on the poet's existence: 'I am – yet what I am, none cares or knows' (1). Clare uses of himself the word 'what' rather than 'who'. 'What' is more impersonal than 'who', and implies that the poet, thinking from the perspective of those who are ignoring him, is imagining himself as merely an object rather than as a subject on an equal footing with those scrutinising him; 'what' therefore turns the poet into an object of impersonal analysis.

The poet laments that his friends have forgotten him, and that he is the only person who observes his sorrow: 'I am the self-consumer

QUESTION

Clare does not use any **dialect** words in this poem. Why do you think this might be?

CONTEXT

It is likely that 'I Am' is written from a personal (or **lyrical**) standpoint and that the speaker is Clare contemplating his mental illness and feeling forgotten by his family while he was in the Northampton General Lunatic Asylum.

of my woes' (3). 'Self-consumer' is a complex phrase and has a number of further possible meanings. It could suggest that the poet is consuming his own woes in the sense of eating them; his woes become part of him, a part of his body and what makes him exist. To consume is also to destroy or to use up; he could be suggesting that he is the person who defeats his sorrows when they 'rise and vanish' (4), and that he is not being helped by his friends in this task. Another reading might draw on a further meaning of 'consume': to engage the full attention of or to dominate; his woes consume him in the sense of them dominating his attention. These woes, we are told, 'rise and vanish in oblivion's host' (4), suggesting that the woes function within the **metaphorical** context of a large number of unspecified things that accompany oblivion (in other words if the state of having been forgotten about could be seen in concrete terms, it would be imagined as large in number because large numbers indicate extremes). Here Clare also gives us a foretaste of the sea **imagery** that is to come in the next **stanza**: 'rise' and 'vanish' hint at waves.

In much of his poetry written prior to 'I Am', Clare is concerned with his fear of being forgotten as a writer. 'Oblivion' is a word he uses often in this context, and these poems frequently refer to being forgotten as being hidden in shadows. The image of the shipwreck is also one that Clare has used before to make the point that the memory of a poet can be destroyed. Clare expresses his concern for the failing reputation of another peasant poet, Robert Bloomfield (1766–1823), in his poem 'To the Memory of Bloomfield' (1823), which compares the pride of assuming that one will remain famous to sailing in 'that gay ship popularity' (2). However, when 'Times wave rolls on – mortality must share / A mortals fate & many a fame shall lie / A dead wreck on the shore of dark posterity' (12–14). Here Clare means that, in time, many people who are famous end up being forgotten by those who come after them. Clare's ambition as a writer often connects with his sense of self, and so it is fitting that in 'I Am' he draws on familiar words and imagery (oblivion, shadows and shipwrecks), previously used in the context of talking about being forgotten as a writer, in order to explore the feeling of being forgotten as a person. The poet concludes the first stanza of 'I Am' with astonishment that in spite of all this pain he still exists.

CONTEXT

Bloomfield's poetry records village life and, like Clare's, uses **dialect**. Bloomfield's *The Farmer's Boy* (1800) sold 30,000 copies by 1803; the first volume of the now more famous *Lyrical Ballads* by Wordsworth and Coleridge (1798) sold 500 copies.

CONTEXT

The fear of being nothing is something that Shakespeare's Hamlet contemplates at a similar moment of emotional extremity: 'O that this too too solid flesh would melt, / Thaw and resolve itself into a dew' (*Hamlet*, I.2.129–30). For Hamlet, becoming vapour would be an escape from the pain of the death of his father and his indecision over how to avenge the death.

The end of the first stanza runs on to the second stanza (**enjambment**) in order to continue the idea of the endless pain of being forgotten and of loving constantly as something that has no real substance. The poet suggests that he lives 'like vapours' that have been 'tossed' (6) into a 'living sea of waking dreams' (8). Clare uses the concept of the waking dream to suggest that the vapours which characterise his state of being are part of a larger body of water that is indistinct in the same way that he feels that he is insubstantial. At the end of the second stanza the poet contemplates the 'shipwreck' of that which he has valued – 'my life's esteems' (10) – and repeats the point made in the first stanza: that even his nearest loved ones seem far away.

The final stanza outlines the poet's hopes. He longs for a quiet and remote place where he can feel close to God. In order to emphasise the remoteness, he suggests that this would be a place 'where man hath never trod' (13) and 'woman never smiled or wept' (14). Here Clare characterises men and women according to traditional gender roles. Men are associated with action; women are associated with emotion. This is a simple and unchallenging world that recalls the Garden of Eden in the Bible. The religious **themes** in the final stanza do not come as a surprise. Clare has already used words that are loaded with religious significance in this poem. 'I am', for example, is what God says to Moses in Exodus when asked what his name is: 'And God said unto Moses, I AM THAT I AM: and he said, Thus shalt thou say unto the children of Israel, I AM hath sent me unto you' (3:14). It is also a phrase used by Jesus in John 14. The phrase is meant to convey the difficulty of understanding what or who God is, and as such has links with the aim of Clare's poem: the exploration of the complexity of identity. There are other words in the poem that appear to be related to messianic themes: those of being forsaken or abandoned (as Jesus was abandoned by the disciples before the Crucifixion), scorned, or involving self-sacrifice (the idea that Jesus gave up his life to save mankind). The religious words imply that the poet is being abandoned to a self-sacrifice (an additional meaning of 'self-consumed') that has a great significance and that will lead him to his 'Creator, God' (15). It is only with the Creator that he will find comfort and a sleep that is 'Untroubling, and untroubled' (17).

CHECK THE POEM

The term 'waking dream' is used by Keats in 'Ode to a Nightingale' (published in 1820), and expresses an important Romantic concept. The Romantics were interested in a wide range of imaginative psychological states; 'waking dreams' were moments of reverie when one could use the physical senses, but at the same time feel that normality had in some way been suspended. The speaker of 'Ode to a Nightingale' asks of the bird's song: 'Was it a vision, or a waking dream? / Fled is that music – Do I wake or sleep?' (79–80).

CHECK THE BOOK

In her 1831 introduction to *Frankenstein* (1818) Mary Shelley writes: 'I began that day with the words, "It was on a dreary night of November," making only a transcript of the grim terrors of my waking dream.'

CHECK THE BOOK

Before beginning *Frankenstein*, Mary Shelley had been reading Coleridge's 'Christabel' (published in 1816): 'A sight to dream of, not to tell!' (l, 253).

CHECK THE POEM

Wordsworth, in 'Intimations of Immortality from Recollections of Early Childhood' (1807), treats childhood as a special state of happiness. Children are closer to nature and lose this closeness when they become adults and, realising that they are not immortal, become aware of death.

CHECK THE POEM

Poet and satirist Jonathan Swift (1667–1745), for instance, writes his own obituary in 'Verses on the Death of Dr. Swift', (1739). Swift's poem observes, humorously, the speed with which his friends and his public will have forgotten him after his death.

The poet's final wish to return to an untroubled sleep is also understood as a return to a childhood peace. Children are often characteristic of happiness in Romantic poetry. The sleep that the speaker of 'I Am' longs for is not in a bed, however; it is outside on the grass beneath the 'vaulted sky' (18). The vault suggests that the world is like a church, and so the religious **theme** is emphasised here, and the wish to sleep on the grass may recall the classical pastoral tradition, where shepherd poets are shown to stretch out in the countryside. It is also possible that this is a wish for death and to be buried in the earth.

GLOSSARY

2	**forsake** give up or withdraw help from
4	**oblivion** the state of forgetting or having forgotten
	host a large number of people or things
5	**throes** violent pains

TO JOHN CLARE

- Clare adopts a detached perspective in order to ask himself whether he is enjoying being at home during the spring.
- His aim is to provide a window on his world.

The speaker of the poem asks the poet how he is, and describes Clare's home in the springtime, full of animal life and activity.

COMMENTARY

Clare addresses himself in this dedicatory **sonnet**. It was written on 10 February 1860 after a silence of about ten years; it is possible, however, that he wrote poetry during this period and that the manuscripts did not survive. Although it is more common to write poems dedicated to other people, it was not unknown for a poet to address himself or herself – usually for the purposes of **satire**. The speaker appears to be a friend asking Clare how he feels now that he is at home and spring has arrived. In reality, Clare was in a lunatic asylum at this time, but his close connection with his home was very important to him, and so it is unsurprising that he writes a poem that imagines what it is like to be home. It is also possible that Clare addresses his son John in the poem. If this is the case, then Clare (as a father) is drawing on the experiences of his childhood home to give the impression of what it must be like for his son.

Much of the poem describes farmyard and wild animals during spring. Birds are 'building nests' (2), the robin visits the pigsty, the old cockerel struts around the hens, the pigs are asleep, and the little boys go bird's-nesting. These are mostly images of different kinds of home: the nest, the sty, the family life of the chickens. Even the unsettling image of boys taking eggs out of nests is reinforced as an image of home, as the boys themselves are on their way back there. The sonnet ends with a comment about the comfort of reading. The boys put their spinning tops and marbles in their pockets while out among the daisies because they are distracted by a magazine that has 'pictures and good stories' (13), such as that of Jack the Giant-Killer.

Clare associates traditional stories, like that of Jack, with the simple honest life. He writes in his 'Essay on Popularity' (1825–37) that while some writers try to be complicated, the best stories are those which circulate among ordinary people:

> children's favourites of 'cock robin' 'little red riding hood' & 'Babes in the wood' have impressions at the core that grow up with manhood & are beloved on poets anxious after common fame as some of the 'naturals' seem to be …

In this essay Clare, concerned with looking at the ways in which writers can achieve fame, comments that the 'naturals' (poets such as Wordsworth and Coleridge) write poems that imitate the simplicity of these traditional folk tales. They, however, 'become unnatural' when they 'seem to be imitating these things by affecting simplicity'. In spite of what he says in his 'Essay on Popularity' Clare admired Wordsworth greatly, but placed a greater value on poetry that came without the need for such a deliberate aesthetic or justificatory stance.

CONTEXT

'To John Clare' was published in the *Stamford Mercury* in 1861. Clare, in a lunatic asylum at the time of writing the poem, did not return to his home before his death in 1864.

CHECK THE BOOK

Clare's 'Essay on Popularity' can be found in *The Prose of John Clare*, edited by J. W. and Anne Tibble (1951).

CHECK THE NET

A version of 'Essay on Popularity' was published under the title 'Popularity in Authorship' in the *European Magazine* in November 1825. You can read a version of this online at **www.johnclare.info** – click on 'Prose'.

CONTEXT

Clare greatly admired William Shakespeare, calling him 'the Glory of the English stage' in his poem 'Shakspear' (1808–19), which celebrates the playwright's accessibility and naturalness.

Clare modifies the English or **Shakespearean sonnet**, dividing the poem into a **sestet** and two **quatrains**. The rhyme scheme is *ababab cdcd efgf*. The punctuation, however, does not follow these divisions, and so the **sonnet** flows easily through the descriptions of the natural scenes, only pausing twice (at the end of line 1 and line 8). Clare balances the formality and discipline of using the sonnet form with the looseness and freedom of minimal punctuation; this use of a loose structure makes the poem seem more natural. Natural-sounding verse is an important Romantic trait, and signals a move away from the rigours of eighteenth-century rule-bound versification.

GLOSSARY

3	**cock robin**	a nickname for a male robin
4	**Ruddy**	red
5	**wattles**	loose flesh on the throat and head of a cockerel or turkey
	comb	the red fleshy crest of a bird, usually a cockerel
9	**bookman**	travelling pedlar
11	**tops**	spinning tops
11	**taws**	marbles
12	**new number**	magazine

CHECK THE POEM

'Song: "A seaboy on the giddy mast"' echoes Cowper's 'The Castaway' (written in 1799), which tells the tale of a sailor who is cast overboard, and survives for an hour before he drowns. Cowper makes the point that his inner turmoil is worse than being cast overboard: 'But I beneath a rougher sea, / And whelmed in deeper gulphs than he' (65–6).

SONG: 'A SEABOY ON THE GIDDY MAST'

- The poem describes a boy on the tall mast of a ship looking at the stormy ocean.
- The focus then moves to the poet, who compares the fear and hopelessness that the boy must feel to his own personal troubles.

A boy on the top of a ship's mast looks out across the sea, which is engulfed in a storm. The poet identifies his mental state with the boy's precarious position, and his troubles with the stormy sea. He compares his own childhood to a bright, sunny morning, which became overcast later in life. He longs to find a refuge from the storm.

COMMENTARY

The first **stanza** of 'Song: "A seaboy on the giddy mast"' comments that the boy sees and hears nothing but the tempestuous waves; the following three give an account of the speaker's emotions. He likens his life to an inconstancy of the ocean waves; hope has vanished for him: 'In every hope appears a grave' (7). Doing his duty to protect the ship by looking out for danger, the solitary boy at the top of the mast is given responsibility beyond his years, sent up the mast because he is small and agile. This central image may draw something from one of the most popular **ballads** of the Romantic period, 'Casabianca' by Felicia Hemans (1793–1835). The reference to the 'giddy mast' (1) also recalls the words of Henry IV in Shakespeare's *Henry IV Part 2* (III.1.18–25). Here Henry, weary, unwell and in the middle of a civil war, longs for sleep and contemplates enviously the many ordinary people who are able to sleep while he, a king, cannot. Sleep, he says, falls on 'the ship-boy's eyes' on the 'high and giddy mast', even though he is in the middle of a storm.

The first line of the third stanza repeats the opening of the second: 'My life is like'. This repetition is known as a **refrain**, and is a common feature of ballads. In this stanza, the speaker's life is likened to the ocean in that it has begun with bright morning sunshine and has since been 'o'erwhelmed' (11) by storms which are 'Deep in the ocean wave' (12). Here Clare may be referring to the inner turmoils he was currently experiencing; the poem was written in 1843, while he was in the Northampton General Lunatic Asylum. The final stanza modifies the refrain by changing the tense. Up to this point the speaker has commented on what his life is like now; in the final stanza he changes to the past tense: 'My life hath been' (13). Here he reviews his life, comparing it once again to a storm at sea. He ends with a question: when will his life be calm again?

The poem uses the traditional ballad rhyme scheme *abab* to build a simple comparison between the view of a boy on the mast of a ship in a storm and the speaker's inner turmoil. Ballads, a poetic form dating back to the Middle Ages, underwent a great surge in popularity after Bishop Thomas Percy (1729–1811) published his historical collection *Reliques of Ancient English Poetry* in 1765.

 CHECK THE POEM

Hemans's 'Casabianca' (1826) tells the story of a boy who remained at his post during the Battle of the Nile in 1798. The poem opens famously: 'The boy stood on the burning deck / Whence all but he had fled; / The flame that lit the battle's wreck / Shone round him o'er the dead.'

 QUESTION

What is the effect of the change of tense in the last stanza?

 CHECK THE BOOK

For more on the ballad revival see Nick Groom's *The Making of Percy's Reliques* (1999). See also Tennyson's collection of 1880, *Ballads and Other Poems*, which includes 'The Revenge: A Ballad of the Fleet'.

The form remained popular throughout the nineteenth century, and is particularly important for the work of Coleridge, Wordsworth, Tennyson and the Pre-Raphaelite poets.

THE PEASANT POET

CHECK THE BOOK
William Howard observes, in *John Clare*, that the final four lines 'contain Clare's most succinct and accurate self-assessment' (1981, p. 150).

- Clare describes the things that are precious to the peasant poet and, by extension, to himself.

This simple **lyrical** poem describes the things that the peasant poet loves. The birds, flowers, weather and insects all remind the peasant poet of God, and are precious to him because of this. The peasant poet is a quiet man, who thinks deeply. His pleasures come from poetry and his woes come from the difficulty of the peasant life. This account describes Clare himself quite accurately.

COMMENTARY

The poem, written while Clare was in the asylum, begins by listing the attributes of the natural scenes that are loved by the peasant poet. Clare uses some description that is conventional, such as the 'cloud-bedappled sky' (4), and some that is surprising. For example, the 'swallow' is described as 'swimming' through the air in line 2. The natural world is beautiful to the poet because of its physical and audible attributes, but it is also a sign of God. To the poet, the noise of the storm is like the powerful 'voice of God' (6). Lines 7–8 of the poem refer to the biblical story of Moses as told in Numbers 20:7–11. Moses has taken the Jews out of Egypt into the desert. Thirsty, his people become angry with him, and so he and his brother, Aaron, go to the door of the tabernacle (the portable shrine used by the Israelites as a sanctuary for the Ark of the Covenant, the chest which housed the scrolls containing the Jewish laws), where God appears to them. God tells Moses to gather his people and his brother, take a rod and speak to a rock. Moses hits the rock with the rod twice and an abundant supply of water comes out. With this **allusion** Clare implies that the rock in the landscape that he loves is as sacred as that which God commanded to produce water. William Blake uses a similar kind of reference in the preface to his poem *Milton* (written and etched in 1804–8):

And did those feet in ancient time
Walk upon England's mountains green?
And was the holy Lamb of God
On England's pleasant pastures seen? (1–4)

CONTEXT
Blake's prefatory poem to *Milton* is now sung as the hymn called 'Jerusalem'.

Here Blake wonders about the truth of the legend that Joseph of Arimathea brought the Holy Grail and the spear that wounded Christ on the Cross to England. His poem ends with the call to build a new Jerusalem 'In England's green and pleasant Land' (16). Clare's allusion does not hint that Moses may have gone to England, but it does suggest that a local rock is as significant to the peasant poet, and to himself, as the rock that God told Moses to command. The religious **theme** continues in lines 9–12, where the poet observes that the peasant poet views everything in the natural world as having been made by God, and loves nature because it is made by God.

The final section of the poem gives a short description of the peasant poet's personality. He is a quiet man, a 'thinker' (14) who follows the average life of a peasant but is special because he has a poet's enjoyment of what he sees and experiences. The description is, to some extent, true of Clare himself. There are hints here of Clare's usual theme of the poet as someone set apart from others: 'A Peasant in his daily cares – / The Poet in his joy' (15–16). This is a prominent theme in Romantic literature, most forthrightly expressed by Wordsworth in his 1800 preface to *Lyrical Ballads*:

What is a Poet? ... He is a man speaking to men: a man, it is true, endowed with more lively sensibility, more enthusiasm and tenderness, who has a greater knowledge of human nature, and a more comprehensive soul, than are supposed to be common among mankind ...

Wordsworth suggests here that while the poet is special – he is someone who possesses a greater ability to communicate – he experiences the same things as ordinary people, but in a more intense way. Clare's idea of the poet suggests that it is his capacity for 'joy' that makes him special.

The first two lines of 'The Peasant Poet' are composed in **iambic trimeter**; Aristotle regarded this as the most conversational **metre**. It is worth noting the use of 's' sounds (sibilants) in the first two lines; these give the impression of the sound of water. The

CHECK THE POEM

Coleridge's 'The Pains of Sleep' (1816) is one of the best-known examples of tetrametric verse.

remainder of the poem alternates between **tetrameter** and trimeter. The rhythm of Clare's poem changes in the last four lines, where the **syntax** prompts each line to divide in half, giving a suggestion of balance. The first part of these lines lists the attribute of the poet; the second elaborates on it. William Howard comments, in *John Clare* (1981), that 'the lack of a verb in the final lines, with its resulting lack of tense' suggests that the poet's assessment applies 'not only to the past but also to the present' (p. 151).

GLOSSARY

10   **brake** thicket

THE ETERNITY OF NATURE

- The poem suggests that the longevity of the self-replenishing natural world will inspire the poet to create verse that will last.
- It describes how nature is eternal – and also somehow mystical.

'The Eternity of Nature' does not tell a story; instead it takes the form of a series of observations about the natural world. Clare lists examples of natural things that will always be there, and suggests that the children of the future will find nature fascinating. The poet finds nature soothing, and it influences the **tone** of his poetry. He is likely to be remembered as a poet, he says, if he can capture his experiences of nature in his poems. He concludes that nature is mysterious.

CHECK THE POEM

William Blake's 'Auguries of Innocence' (1801–5) explores sublimity in the context of the mundane or ordinary: 'To see a world in a grain of sand / And a heaven in a wild flower, / Hold infinity in the palm of your hand / And eternity in an hour' (1–4).

COMMENTARY

The poem, written around 1832, begins with the observation that leaves, which **symbolise** eternity, are simple things when people look at them, but they have a sublime quality and a spirit of their own. By referencing the **sublime**, Clare is **alluding** to a tradition of describing the natural world as something that is awe-inspiring. Typically, dramatic landscapes such as gigantic mountains, huge oceans and large waterfalls are characterised as sublime in the literature of the Romantic period. With the exception of the hills and mountains of the Lake District, Scotland and Wales, sublime landscapes were usually abroad (such as the Swiss Alps). It must be remembered, however, that for Clare somewhere like Scotland would have seemed very distant. He deliberately makes a small and native thing sublime in order to show that one can find beauty and greatness in something that may appear to be very ordinary.

The poet observes that centuries may come and go, but the daisy will still be plucked by future generations. Even though it is small, and often trampled under foot, it is eternal – 'strikes its little root / Into the lap of time' (4–5) – because it will always exist. The as yet unborn child will smile and pluck a daisy centuries from now, even when this poem is as unremembered as a gravestone. When time was a child he ran to pick the daisy in just the same way. This **personification** continues throughout the poem and serves to make the point that time, being young, has many years of life left: 'childish time' (63), for example, loves the songs produced by nature 'like a child' (50) and treats them as his 'play things' (49). We are told that the daisy is such a pretty and feminine flower, with its 'little golden bosom frilled with snow' (19), that even Eve in the Garden of Eden, surrounded by beauty, might pay it some attention and stoop down to show Adam its loveliness. The daisy, 'loving Eve' (23) in return, 'followed' them out of the Garden after the Fall, sharing their sorrow at their banishment. This flower, even though it came from such a glorious paradise, blooms anywhere on the 'blighted earth' (26) and carries on smiling and will do so for ever. It is such a precious flower that Clare calls it a 'little gem' (22). He makes a similar point in 'Song's Eternity', where he also says that 'Nature's universal tongue' (53) sings an 'eternity of song' (51); and in the extract from 'The Parish' quoted in the 1997 Everyman edition he refers to 'our Eden here' (22).

Clare devotes the next section of the poem to the beauties and symbolism of the cowslips and brooks. Like daisies, cowslips, 'time's partners' (30), will continue to bloom in meadows 'when kings and empires fade and die' (29); and brooks in 'green unnoticed spots' (34) will continue to sing when poets are silent and forgotten. Clare's reference to ancient Egypt in his description of the brooks combines the idea of the long distant past with the idea of being forgotten and lost in the confusion of the past. This is not a straightforward statement of forgetfulness, though, as Clare mixes his **metaphors**.

CONTEXT

The most important British source on the sublime for the Romantics was Edmund Burke's *A Philosophical Enquiry into the Origin of Our Ideas of the Sublime and Beautiful* (1757). In this treatise Burke (1729–97) calls the sublime a 'delightful horror'.

 CHECK THE POEM

Keats makes a similar point about the longevity of the nightingale's song in 'Ode to a Nightingale' (published in 1820): 'The voice I hear this passing night was heard / In ancient days by emperor and clown' (63–4).

This section says, literally, that the brooks will continue to sing when poets are forgotten, lying 'in time's darkness' like a mummy in a pyramid (35). But the mummy-like poets 'lie like *memory* in a pyramid' (36, my italics) – so they are more elusive than a body; they are like a forgotten thought. Yet Clare qualifies this by saying that the thought has not been entirely forgotten but has been lost 'Like a thread's end' (38) in a labyrinth. It is then, by implication, findable. The labyrinth image, though not expressed directly, is implied by the words 'in ravelled windings crossed' (38), and also hints at the complex construction of the inside of a pyramid.

The **theme** of the musicality of nature, and its affinity with the musicality of verse, continues in the next section: bees and nightingales will always sing, because 'time protects the song' (40); the robin's song 'lives on' (46) for ever. The poem then takes a more **lyrical** turn when, in line 51, the poet refers directly to himself: 'And so I worship them'. In this significant section, the poet identifies himself as special because 'all else notice not' the natural beauty that he sees (52). Clare's own understanding of how a poet gains inspiration is outlined here: if he touches 'aright that quiet tone' (55) that is to be heard in nature and is a 'soothing truth' (56), then his poetry will achieve longevity: 'still find hearts to love my quiet lays' (58). He will sing for joy like birds flying 'past a crowd' (62) and not in order to achieve 'fame' (59).

The mystic number five (the pentad) is prominent in the final section of the poem. The poet observes that the 'odd number five' (77) occurs in many places in the natural world, which offers the poet the comfort that the world has been designed by God, 'that superior power who keeps the key / Of wisdom, power and might through all eternity' (101–2), rather than by accident. Philosophers call this idea 'the argument from design', and it is one of the well-known arguments for the proof of God's existence. The reference to God and wisdom at the end of the poem takes us back to the Garden of Eden reference earlier, and the poet's stooping to look at the flowers recalls Eve's stooping to look at the daisy. Nature as a mystical force is also seen in 'Shadows of Taste', where Clare refers to it as the 'witchery of bloom' (67).

CONTEXT

A pentangle, or five-pointed star, is seen as a **symbol** of protection in British folklore. It came to Britain via Jewish and Arab culture and was, as Jacqueline Simpson and Steve Roud note, 'reinterpreted in Christian terms as an emblem of the Five Wounds of Jesus, guaranteed to put demons to flight' (*A Dictionary of English Folklore*, 2000). In the medieval poem *Sir Gawain and the Green Knight*, Sir Gawain has a pentangle of 'pure gold' on his shield for protection (620).

GLOSSARY

2	**whereto**	to which
28	**closen**	pasture
54	**bestirreth**	rouses to activity
55	**aright**	in the right way
58	**lays**	songs or poems
67	**sprents**	stains
70	**save**	except
91	**briony**	bryony, a climbing plant with red berries
95	**goosegrass**	scrambling weed with white flowers

SHADOWS OF TASTE

- The poem suggests that taste comes in many forms in the natural world.
- The poet gives us the benefit of his wide experience of the natural world, and concludes that taste is an innate quality that enables us to respond emotionally to nature.

The poem considers the meaning of the word 'taste' by exploring different examples of the ways in which animals and people express preferences for things. Taste is something that is not learned; it exists naturally within certain people. We can see that they have it by their emotional response to the natural world.

COMMENTARY

The poem, which dates from 1830, begins with the observation that there are as many tastes as there are leaves and flowers. Birds express taste in their choice of places to frequent. Some birds live in the short grass, and the yellowhammer prefers to nest beneath 'picturesque green molehills' (10), where shepherds marvel at their strange eggs. The natural scenes that Clare describes in the poem are picturesque (literally 'picture-like'). Although an eighteenth-century aesthetic concept, the **picturesque** continued to be popular in the Romantic period. Picturesque landscapes, natural or man-made, are neither **sublime** nor beautiful, according to this original

CHECK THE POEM

The number five is present in some significant Romantic poems. Wordsworth's 'Lines Composed a Few Miles above Tintern Abbey' (1798) begins: 'Five years have passed; five summers, with the length / Of five long winters!' Coleridge's 'Kubla Khan' (written in 1797 and published in 1816) contains the line 'So twice five miles of fertile ground' (6).

CHECK THE POEM

Clare praises the yellowhammer as 'a poetic model worthy of imitation' in his prose writing, and calls her 'poet-like' (17) in 'The Yellowhammer's Nest'.

CONTEXT

Taste was a popular subject for eighteenth-century essayists. Hazlitt writes in 'On Taste' (1819): 'taste is the power of perceiving ... excellence'. Clare's view is closer to that of Edmund Burke, who writes in *A Philosophical Enquiry into the Origin of Our Ideas of the Sublime and Beautiful* (1757) that taste is extremely hard to describe: 'When we define [it], we seem in danger of circumscribing nature within the bounds of our own notions ... instead of extending our ideas to take in all that nature comprehends'.

definition, but are characterised by their variety, irregularity and complexity, avoiding classical patterns. For example, a gnarled oak is **picturesque** because it is rugged and irregular. The concept was popularised by the work of Sir Uvedale Price (1747–1829), William Gilpin (1724–1804), William Hazlitt (1778–1830) and Richard Payne Knight (1750–1824). Picturesque descriptions are often used in **Gothic** novels, and it is interesting to note that the description of the blasted oak has Gothic elements to it. The ivy is likened to 'straggling ribs' (145); the trunk is 'warped and punished' (143) and is 'Freed from its bonds but by the thunder stroke' (144).

The poet's discussion of flowers is important for the poem as it provides detail for his opinion that they have a range of tastes, and his descriptions demonstrate that he is a man of taste. Flowers in 'Shadows of Taste' seem to be wise and creative, and are blessed 'with feeling and a silent voice' (24). Insects are abundant everywhere and, like the variety of flowers, exemplify the idea that nature has many tastes. They are 'busy' (42) and 'wild' (41) and enjoy many environments; they are so numerous that they have no names. Restless mankind is like a 'noble insect' (45).

People express their taste in lofty ways, in thoughts that 'scale heaven in its mighty span' (46), and in base ways. The 'low herd', by which he means the uneducated, are 'mere savages' (49) who have no feelings or taste and 'Pass over sweetest scenes a careless eye / As blank as midnight in its deepest dye' (51–2). Nevertheless, brilliant minds can spring from among this social group which can 'follow taste and all her sweets explore / And Edens make where deserts spread before' (55–6). Clare uses a familiar image of the natural world as Eden; when nature is viewed with appreciation in his poetry, it is often compared in this way. 'Song's Eternity' describes the 'Melodies of earth and sky' (13) that can be heard in the natural world as 'Songs once sung to Adam's ears' (15), and 'Shadows of Taste' talks of 'Nature's wild Eden' (126).

QUESTION

How does this poem compare with 'Song's Eternity'?

In the section on taste in poetry, the poet makes the point that some people find all their joy in the magic of poetry: in poetry nature 'flings' (59) her beauty over the soul. Taste, **personified**, reads poetry and sees herself there. Poetry immortalises the natural world:

'Dashes of sunshine and a page of May / Live there a whole life long one Summer's day' (65–6). A single moment can be brought to life for ever in a poem. Clare uses the image of a book to show how closely related nature is to writing: May is a 'page' (65); the 'ceaseless' (70) singing bird and laughing brook are conveyed to the 'page of May' in 'living character and breathing word' (72). Here Clare plays on the two meanings of 'character': a letter on a page and the nature or essence of something.

The observation Clare makes here is interesting in the light of Keats's idea, in 'Ode to a Nightingale' (published in 1820), that nature is the superior artist. Keats contrasts the longevity of the bird's song with the failure of his own imaginative attempts to capture such creativity on the page. Much of Romantic poetry is concerned with the lament for the human condition; the sadness of human life makes it harder for us to express our joy and creativity than Keats's 'immortal Bird' (61). Keats suggests in this poem, then, that art can never live up to nature. Clare, however, thinks that nature can be immortalised through verse; therefore the accurate observation of the natural world is crucial to poetry: Clare dubs this the 'true sublime' (77). Accuracy and not **hyperbole** is what leads us to experience the natural world in a heightened state. It is fitting that Clare uses, at the end of the **stanza**, a reference to the Atlas mountains in North Africa, which according to Greek legend supported the heavens.

Referring to styles of poetry, Clare continues with an important **theme** in his work: changes in fashion. Poetry that is 'tawdry' (cheap) or 'chaste' (79), in the sense of tame, has been in vogue. He then lists the ways in which different poets have different ways of writing. The poetry of John Donne (1572–1631) is 'homely' (81), and his rhythms 'Jostle' (82) the reader with impatience. By contrast, Alexander Pope (1688–1744) uses 'smooth rhymes' (83) which are as melodious and regular as a clock. These poets, Clare points out, have influenced the **metrical** choices of later poets: 'From these old fashions stranger metres flow, / Half prose, half verse' (87–8). Clare may have in mind Wordsworth's claim, in the preface to *Lyrical Ballads* (1800), that 'a large portion of the language of every good poem can in no respect differ from that of good Prose'. But, as he admired Wordsworth's verse, it is likely that

CONTEXT

Gilpin's *Observations, Relative Chiefly to Picturesque Beauty* (1772) was particularly important; in it he calls the picturesque a concern with 'endless varieties' and 'elegant particularities'. Price wrote *An Essay on the Picturesque* (1794), while Richard Payne Knight, Price's neighbour and friend, wrote *An Analytical Inquiry into the Principles of Taste* (1805).

 CHECK THE BOOK

Seamus Heaney calls 'Shadows of Taste' a 'verse-essay' ('John Clare: a bi-centenary lecture' in *John Clare in Context*, edited by Hugh Haughton, Adam Phillips and Geoffrey Summerfield, 1994, p. 135).

CHECK THE BOOK
In Jane Austen's *Sense and Sensibility* (1811) Edward Ferrars expresses concern that he cannot use the appropriate terminology associated with the **picturesque**: 'I shall offend you by my ignorance and want of taste if we come to particulars. I shall call hills steep, which ought to be bold; surfaces strange and uncouth, which ought to be irregular and rugged; and distant objects out of sight, which ought only to be indistinct through the soft medium of a hazy atmosphere' (Chapter 18).

the description of the inelegant combination of limping verse and prose that 'Elbows along' (90) is not a description of Wordsworth.

Scientists are the subject of the next **stanza**. The scientist who looks at plants finds treasures that the 'vulgar hinds' (100) or peasants can only understand in the simplest of ways. The scientist is, however, characterised in ways that might be more appropriate for a description of a poet. He finds 'rapture' in the 'simple brook' (99), has 'taste' (107), and 'His joys run riot mid each juicy blade / Of grass where insects revel in the shade' (113–14). The poet laments that the villagers can find nothing in nature 'they as wealth can prize' (104); they can only see in terms of getting richer financially – 'self interest and the thoughts of gain' (105) – and nature, to them, contains no treasures. Here Clare contrasts the wealth of experiencing nature with monetary wealth; he is quite dismissive of the villagers and seems to distance himself from them. Written by someone of a higher social standing than Clare, this would seem to be patronising.

The section continues with the observation that people may think that the scientist is cruel, in that he 'gibbets' (117) butterflies (by this Clare means that he kills them and pins them to boards for display) or 'strangles beetles' (118) in the name of science, but we must realise that this is a noble cause: 'all to make us wise' (118). The end of the stanza reiterates the point that taste is extremely varied, and even though the uneducated may laugh at people who have taste, or stare at them, it is worth observing that those who are so dismissive 'own no soul to look for pleasure' (122) in nature, their feelings are coarse, and they make fun of clever people because they can never be clever themselves: 'Mock at the wisdom which they can't possess' (124).

Those who are interested in wild nature, Clare concludes, forget about conventional beauty, which seems to them to be like a 'withered thought' (148), a dream or shadow. Those who appreciate beauty in nature, rather than wildness, feed their 'spruce and delicate ideas' (153). These people see the picturesque as 'disorder' (154), a 'wilderness of thorns' (155), and prefer gardens that have been designed. They take pleasure in 'gravel walks' (158), plants that have had the benefit of 'gardeners' shears' (156), and nature that has 'art's strong impulse' upon it (160). For Clare, 'art's strong impulse mars the truth of taste' – that is, true taste involves the appreciation of wildness. Clare concludes that these are the 'various moods that taste displays' (161), using an ornate and eighteenth-century style image of enlightenment. Wisdom is like a huge sun and taste spreads out from it in varying rays, radiating from the centre.

CONTEXT

Clare writes elsewhere: 'a clown may say that he loves the morning but a man of taste feels it in a higher degree by bringing up in his mind that beautiful line of Thomsons "The meek eyd morn appears mother of dews"' (*The Prose of John Clare*, edited by J. W. and Anne Tibble, 1951, p. 175). Clare mentions here the great poet of the natural world, James Thomson (1700–48), and his work *The Seasons* (1726–30).

GLOSSARY		
11	**ken**	archaic word for sight or perception
19	**enshrouds**	cover as with a shroud
57	**poesy**	a poetic word for poetry
80	**votaries**	devoted followers
84	**periods**	sequences of musical notes
86	**gamut**	a whole scale of musical notes
98	**furze-clad**	clothed in gorse
100	**hinds**	agricultural labourers
103	**clownish**	peasant-like
109	**lichen**	a fungus that grows on rocks and trees
117	**gibbets**	hangs in the manner of a corpse on the gallows
138	**lea**	meadow
145	**sere**	dry

TO BE PLACED AT THE BACK OF HIS PORTRAIT

- The poem contemplates how immortality is achieved through verse.

Clare writes this poem as a kind of obituary to be placed on the back of his portrait. It is written as a memorial to his poetic interests. He points out that as he loved nature, flowers will live in his poetry and on his grave.

COMMENTARY

The poem, dated 1849, opens with an address: Clare as the 'Bard of the mossy cot' – the poet of the countryside. He immediately picks up the memorialising **theme** here, suggesting that the poet in

CONTEXT

The full title, in Clare's own spelling, is: 'By Clare – To Be Placed at the Back of His Portrate Presented to Inskip by Mrs. Prichard'. Mrs Prichard was the wife of the superintendent of the Northampton General Lunatic Asylum. Thomas Inskip was a friend from Bedford who corresponded with Clare while he was in the asylum.

CONTEXT

The word 'daisy' comes from 'day's eye' or, in Old English, *daeges eage*, because it closes at the end of the day, as if going to sleep. Sleep is often used as a **metaphor** for death, so the idea of the tearful daisy is resonant here.

CONTEXT

The poet's route to immortality through poetry is a popular theme of Shakespeare's **sonnets**. See, for example, Sonnet 55: 'Not marble nor the gilded monuments / Of princes shall outlive this powerful rhyme' (1–2).

the picture is famous – 'Known through all ages' (2) – and has left 'no line to blot' (3), because he has finished writing his poetry. 'Blot' can mean both to stain with ink and to dry the ink with absorbent paper; its primary meaning is likely to be the latter, and implies that there is no more ink to be dried because there is no more writing from this poet. The second part of the first **stanza** gives the reason why the poet has stopped writing: he is dead. Line 5 repeats the structure of the first line, emphasising that this is an address to the bard. Repeated lines and echoes of lines are a common feature of the **ballad**. The dead poet leaves behind him a widow, 'Nature' (8); as a countryside poet, it is appropriate that he should be thought to have married nature. His close association with the countryside is also **alluded** to in the address: 'Bard of the fallow field' (5); 'fallow' suggests that labour has stopped – it is the resting period for a piece of farmland – and it also suggests that the dead poet has stopped his activity.

The second stanza details the natural phenomena dear to the dead poet. He is a poet who loved wild flowers, showers and bracken, but there was nothing dearer to him than the song of the wild bird and the sounds made by cattle and sheep. The first half of the stanza concentrates on visual pleasures; the second focuses on sounds. The final two stanzas are linked together by **syntax**. The third stanza addresses the dead poet as the bard of the 'sheep pen' (17), reiterating the point that he appreciated the beauty of agricultural animals as well as the wild natural scene.

Clare uses the daisy as a mournful **symbol** here, with 'a tear in his eye' (22). Contrastingly, 'The Eternity of Nature' uses the flower as a symbol of happiness. The wren, we are told, arrives in winter (a time traditionally associated with mourning in classical and British literature) and builds her nest in a dry corner of the cowshed. The image of nesting is an image of renewal, and this chimes with the elegiac **tone** of the poem, as **elegies** end on a positive note. Milton, for example, ends 'Lycidas' with the words 'Tomorrow to fresh woods, and pastures new' (193). Shelley's elegy on the death of Keats, 'Adonais' (1821), ends with a similar consolation: 'The soul of Adonais, like a star, / Beacons from the abode where the Eternal are' (494–5).

In the final stanza of the poem the daisy and the wren are both doing hopeful things: the daisy lives both by the bard's grave (or 'bed') and in the pages of his work (31–2). Both 'bed' and 'pages' are **synecdochical** words. The final tribute at the end of the poem takes the form of a command: 'Live on for ages' (30). We are told that the consolation for the poet's death is immortality gained through his work. Nature pays tribute to the dead poet with its gift of flowers, and the flowers also live on in his poetry.

In this poem, Clare links together two ballad stanzas (*abab*) to produce the following rhyme: *abab cdcd*. The punctuation (a full stop at the fourth line of each stanza) emphasises the poem's ballad origins. The **metre**, unlike that of the ballad in its pure form, is irregular throughout, giving the poem a more relaxed feel.

CHECK THE POEM

Flowers are sympathetic mourners in Milton's 'Lycidas' (written in 1637), an elegy in the pastoral form on the death of his friend Edward King (here called Lycidas): 'With cowslips wan that hang the pensive head, / And every flower that sad embroidery wears: Bid amaranthus all his beauty shed, / And daffodillies fill their cups with tears, / To strew the laureate hearse where Lycid lies' (147–51).

GLOSSARY

1	**Bard** a **lyric** or epic poet or singer
	cot cottage
5	**fallow** farmland left uncultivated for a period to allow it to regain its nutrients
12	**bracken** a tall fern
18	**stack yard** farmyard containing stacks of hay
19	**hovel** a shelter for cattle
	glen a mountain valley
26	**pudding-bag** a bag in which a pudding is boiled

MEMORY

- The poet does not want to be forgotten by his friends.
- He wishes to be remembered fondly after he is dead.

CONTEXT

'To be Placed at the Back of his Portrait' was composed during the height of the ballad revival, the beginning of which coincided with the flowering of Romanticism. *The Rime of the Ancient Mariner* (1798) by Coleridge is the most famous Romantic ballad.

The speaker of the poem desires to be remembered, and does not wish to have nature as his only mourner. He would prefer a friend to find his grave and recall happy moments from their friendship.

CONTEXT

This poem is part of the collection Clare called *The Midsummer Cushion*. The meaning of the title was given in a draft preface: 'It is a very old custom among villagers in summer time to stick a piece of greensward full of field flowers and place it as an ornament in their cottages, which ornaments are called Midsummer Cushions'. Midsummer Day is, traditionally, 24 June. The variety of the poems in the anthology echoes the variety of the flowers on the cushion.

CONTEXT

The Midsummer Cushion was not published until 1979, although some of the poems appeared individually elsewhere. 'Memory', for example, was first published in the *Boston Gazette* in 1825.

COMMENTARY

Using a traditional **theme** that goes back to the classics, the poet opines that he does not want it to be his destiny to die like everybody else. The poet Horace, for instance, writes '*Non omnis moriar*': 'I shall not entirely die' (*Odes*, Book 3). Clare's phrase 'I would not' (1 and 3) is repeated for emphasis and means 'I do not want'. The poet does not want his 'humble dust' (3) – his ashes – to be placed in a 'strange' (4) place that is not visited by anyone; by 'strange' he means unfamiliar. Here Clare **alludes** to two of his common themes: the importance of home (he does not want to be transplanted to somewhere with which he has no connection) and solitude (he does not want to be isolated).

There is a tension in this opening, however. Clare is both positive and negative about the commonplace. His ashes are humble, yet he is afraid of being ordinary. Ordinariness is characterised here as the state of being forgotten, as is the 'common lot' of most people (2). The **octave** ends with the poet's wish not to be restricted to having 'nothing save the heedless winds to sigh' (6) for him, and nothing but the morning dew to weep for him. He wants people to mourn his loss. The octave follows the pattern of using repeated phrases – presumably a play on the idea of remembrance and memory. He repeats 'nothing' (6 and 7), 'by all' (5), 'I would not' (1 and 3), and 'unheeded' and 'heedless' (5 and 6).

The **sestet** changes the theme to something more positive. Using the word 'wander' (9), the poet says that he would gladly have a friend visit his grave; 'wander' suggests that the friend's visit is to be spontaneous, informal and heartfelt. The word is unexpected because it suggests directionless movement that has no purpose, and as such it undermines the poet's expressed desire to be remembered. It is, nevertheless, an important word in the Romantic period and is associated with **sensibility**. The poet hopes that the friend will find a path that will lead to where his ashes sleep. He uses here the conventional **metaphor** of sleep for death, and also exploits the metaphoric implications of 'ashes' (10) for the body. The emotional theme continues where the poet says that he will not gain comfort from someone reading his headstone with a 'cold heart' (11). This phrase uses **synecdoche**, the part (the heart) acting for the whole (the whole personality); and **personification**, in that the heart walks past and reads the headstone. Extending the cold metaphor, the poet wishes for someone who can 'keep / Past memories warm' (12–13), and who will remember him fondly and weep for him.

The poem is an experimental **sonnet** that divides neatly into an octave and a sestet yet also has an internal pattern of three sets of **rhyming couplets**, here marked in square brackets: *aba*[*bb*]*ac*[*aa*]*cac*[*dd*]. The octave and sestet division belongs to a **Petrarchan sonnet**, but Clare's poem is very different from the traditional version of this form. Nevertheless, he retains the **volta**.

> **GLOSSARY**
>
> 1   **all** entirely
>
> 2   **lot** fate
>
> 6   **heedless** inattentive
>
> 9   **feign** gladly

EXTENDED COMMENTARIES

TEXT 1 – DECEMBER *FROM* 'THE SHEPHERD'S CALENDAR': CHRISTMAS

First published in 1827, *The Shepherd's Calendar* is in twelve sections (named after the months), each section concentrating on the rural and traditional customs of Helpston, Clare's home village. Clare took his inspiration from Edmund Spenser's *The Shepheardes Calendar* (1579), which was influenced by the classical pastoral tradition. James Hogg (known as 'the Ettrick Shepherd') serialised a similar project in prose in *Blackwood's Edinburgh Magazine* over ten years, beginning in 1819, and published it as a book in 1829. This describes the customs of the people of his native village of Ettrick in the Scottish Borders. Hogg did not, however, organise the text according to months, and it is not known whether Clare knew this work. Leigh Hunt's prose collection *The Months* (1821) and William Hone's *The Every-Day Book* (1825–6) suggest that there was an appetite for this material in the period.

CHECK THE BOOK

Fanny Burney's novel *The Wanderer* (1814) uses wandering to explore the social structures that link women to society. The novel explores the fluidity of identity and the differences between social status and intrinsic worth.

CONTEXT

The idea of walking past the dead without paying sufficient attention to the fate of the person buried may have a biblical context. Lamentations, a book of the Old Testament, reads: 'Is it nothing to you, all ye that pass by?' (1:12).

CHECK THE POEM

The Shepheardes Calendar by Spenser is much more eclectic in style and includes passages of prose, dialogues, various stanza forms and **metres**. Like Clare's poem, it is arranged in sections under the titles of the months.

CONTEXT

The 1997 Everyman edition used in these Notes is based on the manuscript version of the poem, rather than the poem published in 1827. The latter has the stanza beginning 'Old customs' as the final stanza, and the stanza about the yule cake is omitted.

CONTEXT

The custom of decorating houses with holly at Christmas may derive from an earlier Roman custom, while the tradition of kissing under mistletoe became very popular in the late eighteenth century. Jacqueline Simpson and Steve Roud note in *A Dictionary of English Folklore* (2000) that mistletoe became the 'most valued part ... of the elaborate kissing boughs/bushes hung up in farmhouses and kitchens'.

'December' is an early poem, written between 1822 and 1824. In his sketch for it, Clare sums up its structure as follows: 'December – Frost, Snow, Christmas Gambols Winter Sports – Miseries of the very poor – Story'. The poem follows no particular **narrative**; it is, rather, a collection of descriptions and scenes summing up the atmosphere and traditions associated with the month of December, and especially Christmas. 'December' has a regular **stanza** form (*abab cdcd*), which is a modification of the **ballad** rhyme scheme.

In the first scene, Christmas is **personified** and described as having arrived at every home and hearth. Clare returns to personification later in the poem, this time of winter, who is characterised, conventionally, as old and cold. The season is so merry that even 'Old Winter' (33) manages to get warm, wiping away his icicles and warming his fingers until he smiles (33–4). This contrasts with the opening of 'Remembrances', which suggests that when summer pleasures have gone they are replaced by 'the cloudy days of Autumn and of Winter' (2).

In 'Christmas', those who have nothing will dry their tears, we are told, because they are happy at Christmas time. They will crown Christmas with a wreath of holly, even though he may be walking down snowy paths and climbing over stiles covered in frost. On Christmas Eve, every house is swept clean and the windows are dressed with evergreen leaves for luck (evergreens **symbolise** immortality because of their unchanging leaves). Clare picks up on the image of crowning Christmas with a 'holly bough' (4) in the first stanza, and repeats it in the second to suggest that the cottages are made regal by the comfort that Christmas brings. This may refer to the arrival of Christ, who is often characterised as a king, even though he was poor. Further reference to the richness of Christmas is made in the phrase 'Gilt holly' (13).

The scene moves from decoration and preparation to community contentment. Neighbours begin their annual merriment; children go out into the snow and visit their grandmothers to eat Christmas cake. The **theme** of decoration with leaves continues in the next stanza. The ivy-covered ash trees near the cottage farm are often stripped of their branches at this time of year because the cottagers have used them for firewood. The second part of this stanza describes the twisting of hazel branches. Hazel is a flexible wood and was probably used to make the ivy wreaths that decorate the chimney.

In elevated **tone**, Clare addresses these 'Old customs' (41). Here the poet refers to himself and his own preferences for simple traditions. By 'Pride grows above simplicity' (45), he means that pride and arrogance make one spurn simple pleasures. He is concerned that such customs are dying out, and ends the stanza with the observation that the only refuge that old customs (again personified) will have soon will be that of poetry. The memorialising function of poetry is an important theme in Clare's work, and is particularly important in 'The Village Minstrel' (1821). Clare elaborates on the nature of these customs in the seventh stanza. Shepherds become brave and kiss 'giggling' girls (51) because the mistletoe tradition makes it permissible. This is the 'shadow' (55) of a custom because it is a remnant of what was formerly practised; every year, the custom is seen less and less, and 'fashion' (56) causes it to fade. The words 'fashion' and 'shadow' are often used by Clare to indicate that a custom has been or soon will be forgotten.

Music and drama are the subjects of the next section. The carol singers sound like angels amid the noise of the storm, and the peal of the village church bells can also be heard. After the storm, a group of happy people perform morris dances and a winter play. The play allows the 'clown' or peasant to become a king for a short time, and he hopes for 'penny praise' (69) – to be given money. Clare likens the emotion expressed in the performance to a storm, linking this part of the stanza with its opening. His description of the acting – 'The clown-turned-kings for penny praise / Storm wi' the actor's strut and swell' (69–70) – recalls the **tragic** lines in Shakespeare's *Macbeth* (1606): 'Life's but a walking shadow, a poor player / That struts and frets his hour upon the stage … It is a tale / Told by an idiot, full of sound and fury' (V.5.24–7). The clown image is repeated by Clare at the end of this stanza when he describes one of the peasants dressing up as Harlequin.

Clare intersperses the description of winter with things associated with spring and warmth in order to give the impression that it is as warm as May in front of the fire. He says that the flames have a

CHECK THE POEM
'November' from *The Shepherd's Calendar* describes a spectacular storm: 'the slumbering weather flings / Its murky prison round then winds wake loud / Wi sudden start … Storm upon storm in quick succession crowd / And oer the sameness of the purple skye / Heaven paints its wild irregularity' (73–81).

CONTEXT
Harlequin is a character in pantomime. Clare refers to the same kind of character in a letter to William Hone in 1825: he is 'a sort of Buffoon grotesquely dressed with a hunch back & a bell between his legs together with a tail trailing behind him his face blacked and he generally carries in his hand a huge club'.

CONTEXT

Simpson and Roud note that the yule 'block' (81), sometimes called a 'log' or a 'clog', was 'brought in on Christmas Eve with some ceremony, and put on the fire that evening' (*A Dictionary of English Folklore*, 2000). The earliest references to this custom date back to the seventeenth century.

QUESTION

Is the lack of individuality in the description of the rural people a problem in this poem?

QUESTION

Is it surprising that 'December' is a Christmas poem that does not mention Christ directly?

'sunny charm' (90), and the ale is 'flowering' (92) while it warms, and the foam is like cream. Mirth is **personified** as being as happy as 'Summer bees' (93) in a **simile**, and observes the children protected by their parents' knees in an intimate family scene. The children imagine that the snowflakes falling outside are feathers descending from a goose being plucked in the sky. The words 'fancy's', 'superstition's' and 'visions' give an air of the magic of Christmas (100–2). The children also feel as warm as if it were spring.

The **tone** of the poem changes with the introduction of 'Thou' (113), an elevated and archaic form of address. The poet describes Christmas as a day of 'happy sound and mirth' (113) which has long been part of childhood memories. Memory is an important Romantic **theme**. Christmas Day is personified, and the poet remembers having met him 'Harping' (singing) of the 'joys' of present giving (117). The poet laments that the joy of receiving gifts as a child disappears when one reaches adulthood, but recalling them is a great pleasure.

The poem ends by returning to the description of evening pursuits. The cottager reads his Bible, indicating that this is also an important religious festival, and the 'glowing hearth' (137), laughter, drinking and winter stories all sum up Christmas merriment.

GLOSSARY	
6	**rimey** frosty
11	**besomed** swept
15	**deck** decorate
22	**swain** shepherd or farm labourer
23	**crumping** crunching
62	**By fits** suddenly
	steals creeps quietly
75	**wassail** from the Old Norse *vas heill*, 'be in health'; this was a toast which accompanied spiced ale at New Year celebrations
80	**'Christmas box'** it was the custom for the apprentice to collect Christmas tips in his box; this took place on Boxing Day and is origin of the day's name

GLOSSARY		
83	**faggot**	a bundle of sticks
89	**bedim**	make dim or darker
141	**cotter**	cottager
149	**chine**	ribs of beef, mutton or pork

TEXT 2 – *FROM* 'THE PARISH'

This extract is the first two hundred and eighty lines of a longer **satirical** poem, which, in Clare's words, 'consists of a string of characters & farmers of the New & old school a village politician & A Steward a justice of the peace etc etc' (in a letter to James Hessey, 4 January 1823). The **epigraph** is taken from the 'Advertisement' that accompanied Alexander Pope's satirical poem 'An Epistle to Dr Arbuthnot', and is a fitting quotation for Clare, because Pope's poem is concerned with presenting the writer as a shy poet who has found fame but prefers rural retirement. 'The Parish' was Clare's first long poem (at around two thousand lines), and he worked on it between 1820 and 1827. At the time, he thought it was his best poem, writing to John Taylor that it was 'the best thing in my own mind that I have ever written & I mean to take some pains in altering & making it better still if I can' (12 May 1826). Yet Clare could not find a publisher for it, and all of his supporters thought it not suitable for publication because of its political stance. It is an important poem because there are so few poems in this period written by the poor about their poverty. Although poverty is his subject, the poem is largely concerned with class mobility and the effects this has on the culture of the lower classes.

Satire is an unusual form for Clare, who is more interested in **realism** – 'Tell truth' (82) – than in distortion for political effect. For Clare, however, the topic of the poem is both realism and satire: satire must be redefined because what seems to be satire is in fact truth. The poet asserts that if anyone 'but utter what himself has seen' (11) they are accused of being satirical or a political radical. To observe and record the distresses of the rural poor is not, he argues, radicalism; it is merely truth. Those who suggest that poverty does not exist are 'vile flatterers' (15) and 'Patronisers' (25) who speak 'the basest lies' (15) for their own 'self interest' (16); and these are the main subjects of Clare's attack. Clare picks up on Pope's similar rejection of flattery;

CHECK THE BOOK

Mark Storey comments in *The Poetry of John Clare: A Critical Introduction* (1974) that in this poem 'Clare becomes the spokesman for his community: his private anguish is absorbed into the larger more reverberant despair of his fellow countrymen' (pp. 62–3).

Pope describes himself as 'Not Fortune's worshipper, nor Fashion's fool' (334). Clare describes lying in terms of the natural world: liars say that myrtle can grow in winter, that it rains gold, and that winter winds 'blow blessings' (18). To misrepresent the political truth is as ridiculous to the poet as pretending that the natural phenomena he experiences are other than they are.

Pope's attack on flatterers in 'An Epistle to Dr Arbuthnot' is particularly venomous when he talks about Lord John Hervey, a courtier who had attacked him in print. Calling him 'Sporus', Pope depicts him as a jumble of opposites in order to suggest that he is incoherent and unnatural: he is a 'familiar toad' (319) whispering in the ear of Queen Caroline, 'Half froth, half venom' (320). He 'spits himself abroad, / In puns, or politics, or tales, or lies' (320–1). Clare similarly attacks the flatterer – 'Nor can I flatter and I will not lie' (96) – using an image that suggests that he is at once threatening and harmless: 'A spotted monster in a lambkin's hide, / Whose smooth tongue uttered what his heart denied' (27–8). This idea of the commingling of opposites is taken from Pope's poem. In spite of his clear admiration for Pope, Clare attacks **satirists** in his poem. They are hated by everyone, ignorant, self-destructive and 'never missed' (60). Clare **personifies satire** and folly in the second **stanza**. Satire is a kind of gardener whose plants are 'self-interest' (76), and who does not become more civil the more he works. He is not like a barking dog that is quiet when it is fed. He is also the huntsman, who tenaciously goes after his subject. Folly is a 'fool that cannot keep its ground' (83) in a fight; the fool takes offence easily and unnecessarily, and reveals where she is vulnerable. Pope stresses his own honesty in 'An Epistle to Dr Arbuthnot' in order to assert that his satire is well founded and truthful.

Clare's poem, like Pope's, is about public fame. Clare is arguing here that a public reputation at any cost is not worth having: 'A public name's the shuttle-cock of fame, / Now up then down as fashion wills the game' (55–6). Pope uses a similar line to attack Hervey's sexuality, and Clare may be recalling Pope's disgust at Hervey's colourful lifestyle (he had a boyfriend, a mistress and a wife) in these lines. Pope writes of Hervey: 'His wit all see-saw, between that and this, / Now high, now low, now master up, now miss, / And he himself one vile antithesis' (323–5). We can also compare these lines with Clare's description of 'Young farmer Bigg' the **dandy** (239), who is similarly lavish with his attentions, but this time solely towards women: 'Now with that lady strutting, now with this, / Braced up in stays as slim as sickly Miss' (247–8). The above quoted lines from Pope are the only moment in the 'Epistle' where the **couplets** turn into a **triplet** (showing how out of step Hervey is).

Fame is seen in ideal terms in Clare's poem when it relates to the countryside: 'good old fame the farmers earned of yore' (105); by fame he means a good reputation that recommended an individual regardless of their class. He argues that this disappeared once the gentry bought up land for recreational purposes – in particular for hunting and shooting; the 'two sparks' (107) that are fired represent the guns of the huntsmen. The poet imagines a time before class distinctions operated, 'Where master, son and serving-man and clown / Without distinction daily sat them down' (113–14). This egalitarian harmony has now been lost as if it were 'a dream' (117). Traditional pewter tankards once served beer to everyone; now it is **ironic** that the dainty tableware – 'plate' (133) – made by the poor are the things which teach them envy: 'To hate their farms and ape the country squires' (120). The insignia of wealth are now important for the rich: a 'choice patch of pride' (134) – the uniform of the servant – turns the servant into a clown (harlequin), and the liveried footman apes the pomposity of his master.

CHECK THE BOOK

For a good introduction to Clare and an interpretation of his work as politically radical, see John Lucas's *John Clare* (1994).

In two interesting images of women, Clare **juxtaposes** a grand disdainful lady (121–8) with a farmer's daughter. The lady's inherited wealth is what constitutes beauty in the eyes of her husband, who has married her for her money. By contrast, the farmer's daughter 'in days gone by' (143) was beautiful, and able to work outdoors. Now she is as pale and as unnatural as lady's maid, so used to being inside that she can hardly 'dare to venture in the street' (149). Her unnaturalness is also seen in her reaction to nature: she regards people on the street and the winds as 'vulgar' (151). The repetition of 'vulgar' – 'vulgar eyes to shun and vulgar winds' – indicates that she does not distinguish between them and is thus insensitive. The poet regards farmers' daughters, or '"Ladies of the Farm"' (180) as they are pretentiously known, as class traitors. The fault, however, lies with society. People like them are 'taught at school their stations to despise' (153), and the poet is saddened that people like the lady's maid are also taught to 'view

CHECK THE BOOK

Clare's **satire** recalls that of Jane Austen. The vulgarity of Elizabeth Bennet's sisters is used for humorous effect in her social satire *Pride and Prejudice* (1813), while 'Miss Peevish Scornful' (181) also recalls Harriet Smith in *Emma* (1816), who, on Emma's advice, initially rejects a proposal of marriage from Robert Martin, a young farmer, in the hope of marrying higher up the social scale.

CONTEXT

George Cruikshank (1792–1878) drew a satirical cartoon called 'Lacing the Dandy' (1819) in which an overdressed man is being laced so tightly by two servants that his waist is the size of his wrist. He says: 'Fore God ye wretches, you'll never get my stays tight enough'.

old customs with disdainful eyes' (154). They become as prim and unreal as the 'pasteboard figures' that they cut out in school (157); they are vain, taught accomplishments and how to express their tastes. The new farmer's daughter is a mere shadow of the farmer's daughter she has replaced.

Clare's satire on the proud social-climbing women from the 'flimsy class' (239) becomes more focused in the section on 'Miss Peevish Scornful' (181–238), another farmer's daughter. The money her father makes is spent on entertaining her and on making her fashionable, and her head is full of romantic notions about 'Mr So-and-so' (197) and 'young Squire Dandy' (203). The poet is indignant that when Miss Scornful receives the attentions of someone who is her social equal, she is disdainful of him. She waits too long for a proposal from a gentleman, and loses her looks. She sets her sights lower, hoping to marry a farmer, but finally elopes with a servant.

'Young farmer Bigg' (239) receives similar treatment, and is made to look ridiculous. He is used as an example of the kind of man who seduces 'humble' (lowly) 'weak maidens' (253–4). Bigg is duplicitous in that he has neither the wealth nor the social standing that he implies he has. His **dandy**-like appearance suggests that he is somewhat effeminate in that he pays too much attention to the way he looks, even wearing a corset to refine the shape of his figure. It is so tight that he looks like an ill woman: 'Braced up in stays as slim as sickly Miss' (248). Although he is too foolish to be sinister, some of the actions of the dandy farmer or men like him are seen in terms of witchcraft. The maidens who become pregnant are 'As if bewitched, without a father's aid' (258) – in other words it is as if they become pregnant by magic. The whispering that this causes suggests that the farmer's 'deeds are dark' (264), implying that they are evil. This section of the poem is preoccupied with reputation in different ways. The farmer's self-made reputation is false and ridiculous; he is believed by some to be a seducer – 'Thus pointed fingers brand the passing spark' (263) – while his friends believe him to be honourable; and the town thinks of him as a 'proud, conceited, meddling fellow' (268). It is appropriate for someone who thinks so much about his body that those who attempt to ruin his reputation 'brand' (263) him – **metaphorically** burn a mark into his body by pointing at him.

The final **stanza** of the extract uses game **imagery** to make the point that life is unfair. The poet suggests that those who deserve good fortune do not get it, and those who do not deserve it do. Fortune 'deals out wisdom as a curse' (271); reason 'rarely draws' (278) the winning token, only picking out 'Blanks' (279); and the 'prize' is won by 'heedless folly' (280). Clare continues here the **theme** of reputation, arguing that it is usually the case that the poor merit more than their status in life implies. This, of course, has resonance for Clare's own situation as a poor man who struggled for recognition as a man of letters.

 CHECK THE NET

You can view another cartoon by Cruikshank, 'Dandies Dressing' (1818), online: visit **www.pemberley. com** and search for the artist's name and the cartoon title.

GLOSSARY

1	**hind**	agricultural labourer
3	**cant**	jargon belonging to a religious sect
41	**puling**	wailing like a child
45	**cavils**	frivolous objections
51	**bark**	ship
75	**wax**	increase
86	**galls**	makes sore, chafes
108	**coxcomb**	a vain fool
122	**disgusting**	distasteful
127	**lumber rooms**	storage rooms
133	**plate**	gold or silver tableware
159	**glasses**	mirrors
160	**daubs**	ineptly executed paintings
172	**out-Herods**	to act in a manner that is more violent than King Herod, who ordered all of the babies born in Bethlehem around the time of the birth of Christ to be slaughtered (see also Act III Scene 2 of Shakespeare's *Hamlet*)
181	**Peevish**	silly or headstrong
194	**routs**	parties
221	**Gretna Green**	a place in Scotland to which lovers eloped because they could marry legally without a licence, banns or a priest
224	**green sickness**	an anaemic disease associated with women
251	**bemean**	lower in dignity
279	**Blanks**	blank tokens that do not win in a lottery

CONTEXT

Helen Maria
Williams
(c.1761–1827), a
novelist and poet
influenced by the
ideas of the French
Revolution and
who experienced
revolutionary
France herself,
writes of her two-
year absence from
England (in 'A
Farewell, for Two
Years, to England',
1791): 'My native
scenes! Can aught
in time or space /
From this fond
heart your loved
remembrance
chase? / Linked to
that heart by ties
for ever dear, / By
joy's light smile,
and sorrow's tender
tear' (29–32).
Sentiments of this
type are typical in
the **discourse** of
sensibility.

Text 3 – The Flitting

'The Flitting' was written in the summer of 1832, after Clare had been resettled by his friends to a smallholding in Northborough in an attempt to improve his financial circumstances. The move was not a happy one, and Clare felt uprooted from the familiar surroundings of his rural home. Like 'Remembrances', 'The Flitting' voices this disconnection between the poet and the local landscape, and the alienation that has arisen because of an absence of shared history between the poet and his immediate surroundings. Clare incorporates references to his rural location into the poem as memories in a **melancholic** lament. This is an **elegy** for a lost home, but it is also a celebration of the longevity of the natural world.

The subject of 'The Flitting' is homesickness and the crisis that is caused by severing the ties with home. Although he is in fact not very far away, Clare conveys a deeply felt experience of isolation, suffering and exile. But it is not only the poet who is displaced in this poem, for the experience of dislocation is reinforced by the idea that the usual elements of Clare's domestic territory, for example the summer (3), the nightingale (26) and the sun (55), are equally estranged from their environment and disorientated. The title of the poem refers to the action of moving house, but also implies an inconstant, fleeting movement, and can be read as linking directly to the central **theme** of instability, an idea prevalent throughout Clare's poetry.

Clare takes as his starting point the relocation to another place and his recollection of the former home terrain of 'Green fields' (2), 'the hazel's happy green' (5) and 'The bluebell's quiet hanging blooms' (6). The familiar natural elements in the native landscape such as flowers, trees, meadows and wild animals embody the ideal setting, and are now viewed as a lost emotional resource. While the homesick poet recalls the quiet, protective wilderness of home, he evaluates the unfamiliar natural scenery of the new location. Sitting in the same chair (17) but in a different context, he remains constantly linked to home as the new setting gradually comes into focus. Everything seems to be out of place; the sensory stimulation is similar – for example he still hears birdsong – but 'all is strange and new' (21). This is even more so when the poet **alludes** to the nightingale's disorientation as paralleling his own experience of disconnection: 'The nightingale is singing now / But like to me she seems at loss' (26–7).

The source of poetry and the emotional stimulation of the heart are located in the home landscape (31–4). The thoughts of home do not, however, alleviate the feeling of solitude: 'Alone and in a stranger scene, / Far, far from spots my heart esteems' (49–50). Aware that such isolation and alienation brings with it a childish inwardness, the poet returns to his thoughts of home which surface in his mind, growing 'like weedlings wild' (59). The recovery of these thoughts, and his immersion in these images of home, is deemed necessary because without them his poetry would be devoid of joy and pleasure (61–4).

The poet turns to books as an alternative source of happiness and joy but finds that their cultural fashions are unfixed and changeable: 'I read in books for happiness / But books are like the sea to joy' (65–6). Clare sets up a contrast between the high culture of the educated on the one hand and the low culture of the uneducated on the other. He suggests that the act of educating himself by reading would cause the rustic and untutored poet to disregard the natural world that he has always held in high esteem (69–70). Books which tell of 'the pomps of chivalry' (73) and 'legends of the ancient time' (74) represent high literary culture; they present rich, mysterious stories of 'gold and pearls' (75), and offer a form of 'sublime' (76) which inspires merely a painted shadow, in other words obscured and artificial. According to the poet, the true location of the **sublime**, which inspires a feeling of awe and wonder, often at the sight of an overwhelming natural landscape, is to be found in 'plain and simpler things' (78) – by this Clare means in the direct experience of the ordinary in the natural world.

The shadow **motif** is introduced again in an **allusion** to the 'Vague unpersonifying things' (90) currently present in the unfamiliar surroundings of the poet's new landscape. This suggests that he cannot focus well on the features of this country scenery, which neither comes to life nor displays human characteristics. The crux of the problem is that the poet's **psyche** is still connected to his home. On one level there is an interweaving of the new and old landscapes, but the new landscape serves only as a backdrop for emotional disorientation, and is a place in which he has no history (97–112).

In contrast, the perfect Eden that is the old landscape is exemplified through his ability to communicate with the plants and animals

> **CONTEXT**
>
> The nightingale is an important **symbol** of creativity and happiness in Romantic poetry. Coleridge calls it 'the merry Nightingale' (43) in 'The Nightingale' (*Lyrical Ballads*, 1798); Keats observes that the bird is 'too happy' (6) in 'Ode to a Nightingale' (published in 1820).

(121–8); this shows that no distance existed between him and the natural world. These natural elements are constants, and are revealed as having inhabited this landscape since time immemorial; they are 'All tenants of an ancient place / And heirs of noble heritage' (129–30) and are 'Coeval' (131) with, or existed at the same time as, Adam, the first man. The message here is that when the poet sees such flowers, he feels part of a chain of natural life which has existed from the time of the creation of the world (129–36). The majesty of this natural scene is enhanced by references to coronations and kings: the long succession of kings in China (139), the flowers that 'crowned wilderness and rock' on the first day (146), the story in Genesis of Abel.

Clare places his disregard for the conceited grandeur of 'highflown fangled things' (153) and 'haughty pomp' (154) in direct opposition to these benign and mostly biblical examples. He neither seeks out the Muses of the classical tradition for inspiration, nor tries to create images of architectural splendour by imagining great cities stretching into the distance as far as the eye can see (157–60). His preference is for simple rustic verse that is 'mild and bland' (161), and his muse should be a patron of 'native poesy' (164). Clare is not interested in his muse's power to inspire, but rather her ability to empathise with his local environment. He visualises her as a figure like himself, walking with admiration through his native landscape, and experiencing great joy at the natural sights (163–72). As a rustic muse she would count the eggs in the moorhen's nest in the reeds, and long to learn the lessons of the natural world (173–5). She would not mind staining her gown when sitting on molehills, and would not praise the songs of flowers that she had never seen (177–84). Her reactions to his landscape indicate that she is a kindred spirit.

In the final section of the poem Clare focuses again on his feeling of being displaced from home. This grief for the loss of his home causes him to become attached to the 'simple weed' (186) and the wild plant, the 'little "shepherd's purse"' (187). He realises that these plants are native to his new home as well as to his old (185–92), and are a part of his memories. For Clare, the weeds are an image of continuity and stability, and have a secure place in the ancient natural world. In line 59 the weeds are compared to thoughts which have staying power, and return to blossom in

CONTEXT

Abel was the second son of Adam and Eve and was a shepherd. Clare combines the biblical story of Abel dedicating the firstborn sheep of his flock to God (147–8), mentioned in Genesis 4:4, with the garlanding customs associated with May Day.

www. **CHECK THE NET**

To see pictures of shepherd's purse and find out more about this little plant, type 'shepherd's purse' into an Internet search engine.

'places known so long' (61). Although not grand elements in the scheme of things, the 'Poor persecuted weeds remain' (212) and 'the grass eternal springs' (215) after the destruction of 'old marble cities' (211), and when grand castles stand in ruins (216). Constancy is found in the natural world of the local setting, and not in the built environment or the world of palaces and kings.

GLOSSARY		
11	**besom**	broom
	ling	heather
	teazle	prickly leaved flowering plant
	burrs	seed pods on a prickly plant
23	**puddock**	a buzzard
45	**shelvy**	like shelves
51	**closen**	small enclosed fields
99	**swee**	swing
105	**shoaf**	sheaf
107	**stowks**	bundles of straw
115	**conned**	known
131	**Coeval**	of equal antiquity with
137	**lambtoe**	bird's-foot trefoil, a small plant with yellow flowers
147	**May**	hawthorn blossom
168	**sallows**	willows
172	**a naiad**	a water nymph in classical mythology

CONTEXT

Royce Wood (24, 28), also known as Rice Wood, was one of Clare's favourite haunts, and was home to many nightingales.

PART THREE

CRITICAL APPROACHES

THEMES

NATURE AND ENCLOSURE

Clare is, primarily, a poet of place. He records in tremendous detail the specifics of the flora and fauna of his home, concentrating on the changes in the seasons (see 'The Nightingale's Nest' in **Detailed summaries** and 'The Flitting' in **Extended commentaries** for good examples). He is also interested in the impact of politics on the landscape. Several key **symbols** emerge in his nature poetry: the nest, enclosed land, flowers and birds.

CHECK THE BOOK

Clare's prose reveals his interest in nature too. He writes in a letter on natural history that the wren 'finds its food in stackyards & builds its nest mostly in the roof of hovels & under the eaves of sheds about the habitations of man tho it is often found in the cowsheds' (*The Natural History Prose Writings of John Clare*, edited by Margaret Grainger, 1983, p. 53).

The nest stands for an image of home. Jonathan Bate writes in *The Song of the Earth* (2000) that many of Clare's nest poems recapture 'the wonder of the child finding a nest, but [he] also recognizes the vulnerability of the nest, which becomes an analogue for the vulnerability of his own being-in-the-world' (p. 158). In other words, the nest is a **metaphor** for vulnerability because it is so small and fragile. Clare comments on the **irony** of the nest that is unexpectedly at ground level, such as that in 'The Skylark' and 'The Landrail'; this kind of nest is safest from young boys in search of eggs. The yellowhammer's nest is not, however, safe from snakes. In encounters with the nest, Clare often describes the speaker bending down to its level. 'The Pettichap's Nest' is 'on the almost bare foot-trodden ground, / With scarce a clump of grass to keep it warm' (4–5); it is important for him to be close to it as this removes all boundaries. 'I stoop for many' (98) he says of observing flowers in 'The Eternity of Nature'. The nest is significant because it is a secret place too; the pettichap's nest is 'Hard to discover' ('The Pettichap's Nest', 20). Clare is interested in looking at the nests, but not in disturbing them or possessing them. In 'The Pettichap's Nest' he says to his companion: 'We'll let them be and safety guard them well, / For fear's rude paths around are thickly spread / And they are left to many dangers' ways' (27–9). This is his attitude, generally, to the natural world. In spite of the beauty that he observes in 'Sonnet: "I dreaded walking where there was no path"', there is great personal consolation in not owning anything: 'having nought I never feel alone' (13). The nest, then, is both a place of safety and a place that is at risk. Horses may 'trample' past the pettichap's nest 'twenty times a day' (34), but 'like a miracle in safety's lap / They still abide unhurt and out of sight' ('The Pettichap's Nest', 35–6).

The enclosure of fields is a painful subject in Clare's work and stands for the unacceptable boundaries put up by the government to convert public into private land, which, in Clare's opinion, equalled hardship for the poor and the loss of the freedom to wander (for more on enclosure see **Historical background**). 'The Lament of Swordy Well' is spoken from the perspective of an overworked and plundered piece of land that, the poem says, feels enslaved like the rural poor. 'The Moors' explores the wild ground 'Bespread with rush and one eternal green' (2). The land has never been ploughed and stretches out into the horizon without a boundary: 'Its only bondage was the circling sky' (10). We can see the link with 'The Lament of Swordy Well' here in the slavery image. Clare is often very explicit that enclosure ruined the landscape aesthetically as well as having sad consequences for those who used the land for grazing, as they had no private land of their own. 'Enclosure came and trampled on the grave / Of labour's rights and left the poor a slave' (19–20) he writes in 'The Moors'. The land has been chopped up into small parts for people who cannot understand anything as noble as common ownership:

> And sky-bound moors in mangled garbs are left
> Like mighty giants of their limbs bereft.
> Fence now meets fence in owners' little bounds
> Of field and meadow, large as garden grounds,
> In little parcels little minds to please (45–9)

The 'bounds' or boundaries are small and petty. The word 'destroyed' is repeated in this poem and the moor seethes with anger and concern. Signs saying '"no road here"' (70) are placed on ivy-covered trees as if they are telling the birds not to go there. The poor, he says, have no voice: 'much they feel it in the smothered sigh' (76), but experience its loss deeply. Using an **oxymoronic** and **alliterative** phrase, Clare characterises the incomprehensibility of this offence to the land and the people as 'lawless law's enclosure' (78).

In 'The Village Minstrel' (1821) Clare observes that enclosure is powerful enough to change the seasons: 'Spring more resembles

CHECK THE NET

An excerpt from *The Enclosure Maps of England and Wales 1595–1918: A Cartographic Analysis and Electronic Catalogue* by Roger J. P. Kain, John Chapman and Richard R. Oliver (2004) gives a good introduction to the history of enclosure: visit **http://assets. cambridge.org** and search for the short title.

winter now then spring' (1082). Enclosure is seen here as the instrument of 'oppresions power' (1071) that has caused a major deterioration in the natural world, and the death of customary events. The peasant poet, Lubin, is consoled after enclosure has damaged the landscape by remembering the village life that has passed. Enclosure also damages the correct relationship between the people and the natural world, as we see in 'The Moors'. For the speaker in 'The Fallen Elm' (1830), enclosure, **personified**, is guided by 'ruin' (57). The cottage which the elm sheltered is made into 'workhouse prisons' (60) where the poor are made to go as a consequence of the law that caused the tree to be felled. The poems about enclosure are often called the enclosure **elegies**, because of their mournful **tone**.

Another feature is Clare's extensive use of Edenic and **golden age imagery** in his nature poems. The cycles of the natural world make it long-lasting; 'The Eternity of Nature' explores the mystical quality that this self-renewal implies. Poetry has an important role in helping the reader to acquire the taste to appreciate nature. As he writes in 'Shadows of Taste', in poetry 'nature o'er the soul her beauty flings / In all the sweets and essences of things' (59–60). His exploration of this **theme** continues in 'Song's Eternity', in which nature sings **ballads** that are 'six thousand years' old (17). Contemplating nature's eternity leads Clare to metaphysical subjects occasionally. He sees God in 'The Eternity of Nature' as a transcendent creator with 'superior power' (101).

CHECK THE POEM
Clare's **sonnet** 'Earth's Eternity' is worth looking at in the context of nature's eternity.

Aspects of the natural world are frequently **anthropomorphised** in Clare's work. Birds are usually female, as in 'The Wren' and 'The Nightingale's Nest'; they are happy or solitary; and they share sympathy with the speaker of the poem. The yellowhammer is capable of a broken heart; and ants are capable of social behaviour, as the sonnet 'The Ants' reveals. In 'The Lament of Swordy Well' the 'piece of land' (21) sings its own elegy as if it is alive; the 'Old Elm' (1) in 'The Fallen Elm' murmured 'The sweetest anthem Autumn ever made' (2) and is a 'Friend not inanimate' (29); and the 'landscape laughs in Spring' (1) in the sonnet of the same name. By contrast, Clare sometimes describes people in terms of animals.

Miss Peevish Scornful in 'The Parish' apes her betters; the boys in 'The Skylark' wish to be like the bird; the cottager in 'The Cottager' 'Rests with the lamb and rises with the lark' (100); and the 'mongrel men' cause the 'strife' (198) of Swordy Well in 'The Lament of Swordy Well'.

Nature also has a comforting effect on the speakers of Clare's poems. In 'The Fallen Elm', for instance, the tree's 'seasoned comfort' (11) entered the hearts of the family in the household next to which it stood, and the poet describes his 'friendship' (28) with the tree. However, the interaction between people and nature is often destructive, Clare observes. People are 'spoilers' (62), he writes in 'The Fallen Elm', with 'vile unsatiated maws' (73). In this poem we move from a domestic description of the joy that the tree brought to the political significance of its demise, and the consequences for the poor: it becomes a political **symbol**. Nevertheless, Clare makes much use of the idea of rural retirement, a great eighteenth-century and Romantic theme (see **Melancholy, sensibility and madness** below).

VILLAGE LIFE

The record of village customs, agricultural practices, songs and stories is at the heart of Clare's poetic mission. Clare wanted these customs to be preserved, and to register his protest at the causes of their decline. His aim was to write about his local environment. As John Barrell observes in his 1972 work *The Idea of Landscape and the Sense of Place 1730–1840: An Approach to the Poetry of John Clare* (p. 120):

> Clare's writing after 1821 or so is increasingly preoccupied with being 'local', and … he is concerned with one place, Helpston, not as it is typical of other places, but as it is individual; and individual not because it is different, but because it was the only place he knew: nature may well have been the same elsewhere as in Helpston, but Clare was only familiar with nature as it was in his own parish.

Clare's subject was a life that he knew well, and the memory of this life sustained him while he was imprisoned in the lunatic asylum.

 CHECK THE BOOK

In *The Country and the City* (1973) Raymond Williams suggests that nostalgic descriptions of England should not be taken literally, but as linguistic creations. He describes rural communities, such as that portrayed by Clare, as remnants in some ways of an older cultural system working in opposition to the dominant culture. Nevertheless, he believes that the idea of the rural community has been incorporated into the notion of leisure for the dominant class.

In 'December', in *The Shepherd's Calendar* (1827), Clare concentrates in detail on the recreational life of a community. The celebrations are centred on community cohesion. Men kiss women under the mistletoe because custom allows them to, and people sing and dance together. Clare is explicit about the kinds of food and drink that are consumed, and even goes into detail about how they are prepared. His eye focuses on a range of moments that are typical but not part of a general experience, for example the way the inside of the windowpanes have misted up, and the curl of the flames of the fire which is warming the jug of foaming ale. These are, then, individual experiences as well as typical ones.

Clare is drawn to traditions that have a long history. 'December' mentions morris dancing, a tradition often associated with May Day celebrations, and distinctive in that the dances are only performed on special occasions. Brightly coloured costumes, face paint and masks are features of morris dancing, and there are many regional variations. Clare describes morris dancers as 'Bedecked in masks and ribbons gay' (66). He writes in a letter to William Hone's *Every-Day Book*, a collection of articles about the customs associated with each day of the year, in 1825, that 'The Morris Dance is very popular now with us[;] they begin to go round the week before Christmas'. Clare was anxious to connect with antiquarians who were also preserving these customs in print. 'St Martin's Eve', similarly, explores the customs of the community, stressing community cohesion, with the exception of the fallen woman, 'once-beguiled Kate' (113). Even though Kate is on the margins of the social group depicted, she is **ironically** at the heart of the custom, for it is she who follows the St Martin's Eve ritual of placing an onion under her pillow.

'The Parish' (1820–7) explores the threat to peasant culture posed by land enclosure. The poem shows a society that has had its values changed. The simple pleasures of the rural way of life have been replaced by pretentious behaviour and unnatural people. The kind of equality that meant that peasants sat down to eat with those of a higher social standing has faded away. Instead the peasants 'ape' them (120), and thus they make themselves ridiculous. Clare is asserting here that enclosure throws peasant culture into disarray, destroying the dignity and protection that the poor have enjoyed. The character sketch of the farmer's daughter, who has been

---

CONTEXT

Morris dancing was originally a dance by Moors or Africans ('morris' is a corruption of the word Moorish) and was brought to Britain from Spain in the reign of Edward III (1327–77).

CHECK THE POEM

Working on the land himself, Clare recorded different activities concerned with agriculture and farming in his poems. See 'Sonnet: "The barn door is open"', 'The Wheat Ripening' and 'The Beans in Blossom'.

educated to be a lady, emphasises the unnaturalness of this class upheaval. She is without beauty or grace, and lives a wasteful and unproductive life. Clare presents customs, in this context, through **satire**. Old and meaningful actions are replaced by empty ones that are not genuine and do not belong to the class of people that perform them. They are empty reflections of a need to social climb that Clare finds objectionable.

POETIC FAME AND LITERARY FASHION

Clare explores the concept of poetic fame (in other words what it means to become famous through writing poetry) through looking at his own experiences of entering into the world of publication. Some of these poems, such as 'The Village Minstrel' (1821), follow the fortunes of fictional peasant poets, and others consider the effects of fame in more abstract ways. Clare is also concerned with the damage done to poetry by literary fashion.

For Clare, like Wordsworth, the ideal poetry is that which is sincere; but in the case of Clare, sincerity is achieved when the 'unconscious poet of little name [who] writes a trifle as he feels without thinking of others & ... becomes a common name' ('Essay on Popularity', 1825–37). By the phrase 'common name', Clare indicates that he admires the kind of fame that does not involve the commercial world. Commercial success in writing, he argues, is the route to obscurity. Similarly, poets who aim for the current fashion are likely to be forgotten sooner than those who aim to express themselves in a more sincere way. 'Common' fame is something that has been achieved by popular stories, such as that of 'Little Red Riding Hood' and 'Babes in the Wood', and by traditional **ballads** that have no traceable author. 'The ballad in the ploughmans pocket wears / A greater fame then poets ever knew' ('The ballad in the ploughmans pocket wears', 1832–7).

The concept of common fame appears often in Clare's poetry. When he discusses it, he often describes it in terms of oral culture. Traditionally poetry was sung; it was recited and delivered by bards who had learned the words by heart. This was particularly important in a culture where reading was not widespread, and still persisted in Clare's time: Clare recalled his father telling him stories in this way.

> **CONTEXT**
>
> The aim of *Lyrical Ballads*, as Wordsworth put it later in his preface of 1800, was to 'choose incidents and situations from common life, and to relate or describe them, throughout, as far as was possible in a selection of language really used by men'. He and Coleridge were inspired by the ballad revival initiated by Thomas Percy's *Reliques of Ancient English Poetry* (1765).

POETIC FAME AND LITERARY FASHION continued

CHECK THE POEM

Poetry written by the uneducated had been in vogue for a long time. Stephen Duck gives an account of a thresher's life (someone who separates grain from straw) in 'The Thresher's Labour' (1736): 'With rapid Force our sharpen'd Blades we drive, / Strain ev'ry Nerve, and Blow for Blow we give. / All strive to vanquish, tho' the Victor gains / No other Glory, but the greatest Pains' (116–19).

Clare was very dismissive of literary fashions. Commercial popularity is 'superficial' and 'branded', he suggests in his 'Essay on Popularity', and it interferes with the integrity of the poet. Poets of the day may be 'very slender names come to be popular from many causes with which merit or genius has no sort of connection or kindred' and commercial fame is transient. This **theme** is taken up in 'The Parish', where the poet observes that his own verse is at odds with what is acceptable: 'I envy not their praise' (47). He does not want to be a 'cur that licks' (35) the shoes of his patrons, only to be soon forgotten, as 'A public name's the shuttle-cock of fame' (55). Far more appropriate is the 'good old fame the farmers earned of yore' (105).

Clare's understanding of how poetry should be written, in privacy, with sincerity and with scant attention to literary fashion, stems from his reluctance to enter the public world. Unusually, when Clare talks about commercial publicity, he uses images that are more appropriate for an oral culture. False fame or commercial fame, he suggests, is like an echo 'delaying / When he that woke it into life is vanished' ('Fame', 9–10). The orality of this image of fame undermines it, making it seem less substantial than it really is. He often compares fame to shadows. 'Song's Eternity' asks whether 'Pride and fame must shadows be?' (43).

Clare began writing poetry for his own amusement, but was driven to consider publishing it when his financial situation became dire. His earliest poems were written for his parents and were meant to be private. The sincerity that is a marker of his poems can be seen in his attitude towards his parents' literary taste: 'if they coud not understand me my taste shoud be wrong founded' (*Autobiographical Writings*, edited by Eric Robinson, 1983, p. 12). Although he clearly trusted the judgement of his parents, he kept his authorship of the unpublished poems he read to them secret: 'I … wrote my pieces according to their critisisms, little thinking when they heard me read them that I was the author' (p. 12). Embarrassment, caused by pursuing an activity that was unusual for a labouring man, is also part of the reason why Clare wanted to keep his authorship secret (*Autobiographical Writings*, 1983, p. 82):

I felt ashamd to expose them on paper and after I venturd to write
them down my second thoughts blushd over them and [I] burnt
them for a long while but as my feelings grew into song I felt a
desire to preserve some and usd to correct them over and over till
the last copy had lost all kindred to the first even in the title

When he had finished writing his poems, Clare hid them in an old
unused cupboard. A local bookseller, Edward Drury, gave Clare the
opportunity to relieve his financial distress by publishing his poetry.
Drury had good literary connections (he was cousin to a London
publisher, John Taylor), and he encouraged Clare's writing, giving
him financial assistance. We see Clare's embarrassment again in
'First Love's Recollections', in which Clare reveals that he still loves
Mary Joyce: 'My words e'en seem to blush for shame / That own I
love thee on' (43–4). It is sweeter to him that his poems were loved
by her than by any wider public: 'Ere the world smiled upon my
lays, / A sweeter meed was mine' (57–8). Her response, like Clare's
own, is blushing: 'Thy blushing look of ready praise' (59).

Clare's early poetry is preoccupied with the problem of public
authorship. In his untitled and unpublished poem 'No hailing curry
favouring tothers Muses' (1819) Clare attacks enforced insincerity
that aims to please fashion and patrons. Here, in **lyrical** mode,
Clare looks back to the regal contentment he felt 'while earning /
A shilling mong my neighbours / Unknown to books unknown to
learning', when 'peace then crownd my labours'. In 'Song's Eternity'
(1832), Clare questions: 'Can it be / Pride and fame must shadows
be?' (42–3). Poetry that is authentic, however, is long-lasting:

Songs once sung to Adam's ears
Can it be?
– Ballads of six thousand years
Thrive, thrive, (15–18)

Clare doubts that he will achieve common fame himself. While
ballads will be sung for eternity, books are 'Trifles unto nothing
wed' (29). Although Clare's poetry was fashionable for a short
while, his aim was not to become fashionable. It happened that
the kind of poetry that he wrote was popular at the time.

> **CONTEXT**
>
> Duck (1705–56),
> known as the
> thresher poet,
> came to the notice
> of Queen Caroline,
> wife of George II,
> who gave him a
> pension. In 1756
> he drowned
> himself during
> a bout of
> depression.

**CHECK
THE POEM**
Coleridge's
'Dejection: An Ode'
(written in 1802)
describes depression
as 'A grief without
a pang, void, dark,
and drear, / A
stifled, drowsy,
unimpassioned
grief, / Which finds
no natural outlet,
no relief / In word,
or sigh, or tear'
(21–4).

 **CHECK
THE POEM**
John Keats's 'Ode
on Melancholy'
(published in 1820)
is an important
Romantic
exploration of the
subject. Keats's
speaker begins by
attempting to resist
his depression: 'No,
no, go not to Lethe'
(1), and as he feels
himself drawn
down, he suggests
that one should
make the best of it.
'But when the
melancholy fit
shall fall / Sudden
from heaven like
a weeping cloud'
(11–12), then one
should treat it
as an indulgence
and see its beauty.
Melancholy is
transient, he
concludes, though
one is defeated by it.

MELANCHOLY, SENSIBILITY AND MADNESS

Melancholy is a major element of the emotional landscape of
Clare's poetry, and was an important topic for Romantic poets. The
anxieties that reveal themselves in Clare's initial attitude towards
authorship – that it was fundamentally better for it to be private –
remained with him throughout his life. His disposition was clearly
towards **melancholy** or what would now be called depression.
In particular, Clare found change very difficult. As Mark Storey
comments in *The Poetry of John Clare: A Critical Introduction*
(1974, p. 9), the stressful changes in Clare's life took several forms:

> the enclosure of his native village, unexpected fame, neglect,
> marriage to the girl he had made pregnant, the loss of his
> childhood love, Mary Joyce, moving house in 1832 (only three
> miles, but too far for Clare), confinement in first one asylum
> then another.

Storey argues that Clare's poetry is a search for stability. He
searches his past experiences in order to gain consolation from
change, and 'he hopes to challenge the processes of change' (p. 9).

Connected to this is Clare's wish for isolation, a central **theme** of
many of his poems, and often linked to his anxieties over achieving
literary fame. 'Summer Moods' (1830), for example, follows the
tradition of **retirement literature**, popular in the seventeenth and
eighteenth centuries. Here the speaker loves 'at eventide to walk
alone' (1). Retirement literature celebrates the virtues of the quiet
life of the countryside in contrast with the bustle of the city, and has
its origins in ancient classical poetry. Alexander Pope (1688–1744),
the eighteenth-century **neoclassical** poet, composed the following
lines in celebration of the quiet life: 'Happy the man whose wish
and care / A few paternal acres bound, / Content to breathe his
native air / In his own ground' (1–4). Pope's poem, 'Ode on
Solitude' (written *c*.1700), suggests that rural retirement is the route
to happiness, and ownership of one's own land is also important.
The close connection between contentment and a sense of belonging
is also explored by Clare, and his 'Sighing for Retirement' (1840–1)
is very much in this tradition. Here the poet asks to be taken away
from the noisy 'busy crowd' (1) and to be returned to the natural
world with its 'quiet joys' (4). He finds his 'poems in the fields' (15),

and 'only wrote them down' (16). Retirement to the countryside is beneficial for poetry. Clare was also influenced by James Thomson, Thomas Gray and William Cowper in this.

Melancholy also features in the literature of **sensibility**. Sensibility is a refined kind of emotion – in the eighteenth and nineteenth centuries, experiencing this emotion indicated that person had good taste and was passionate. Sensibility permeated all literary genres during the Romantic era: the novel, **Gothic** literature, the essay, poetry, drama. It began as a way of expressing philanthropic compassion and humanitarianism, but towards the end of the eighteenth century and the beginning of the nineteenth century, many writers (for example Jane Austen in *Sense and Sensibility*, 1811), began to **satirise** its excesses, depicting sensibility as emotional indulgence and selfishness. Stuart Curran observes in *Poetic Form and British Romanticism* (1986) that 'Where the Renaissance had played its variations on the ecstasies of love and religion, the later eighteenth century reared its monument to unavailing sorrow. Sonnets of sensibility flooded forth like tears' (p. 30).

Sensibility is manifested in British literature in a number of ways. The language of sensibility quickly became conventional in eighteenth-century literature. Key words such as 'benevolence', 'pity', 'compassion', 'sincerity', 'virtue', 'terror', 'horror', 'enthusiasm', 'melancholy', 'reverie', 'sympathy', 'spontaneity' and 'transport' are frequently used. In general the language is **hyperbolic**. Emotions 'swell' and 'overflow' – and there is much emphasis on their infectiousness. We can see an example of Clare using the language of sensibility (or sentimentality) in his more personal poems such as 'Love and Memory'. The inexpressibility of grief, for example, in this poem expresses the poet's sensibility:

> And now thou art from me
> My being is gone.
> Words know not my grief
> Thus without thee to dwells (83–6)

Clare's madness, or alleged madness as some have preferred to call it, has received much critical attention. Clare spent more than

CHECK THE POEM

Tennyson's *In Memoriam* (published in 1850, begun in 1833), is a Victorian exploration of melancholy and the grief of losing a close friend. Clare's 'Melancholly' (1832) calls the condition an 'illness' which 'benumbs' and hunts us 'like a tiger hunts his prey'.

twenty-five years in the asylum, paid for by a subscription fund. At the end of 1821 Clare began to talk of his condition as caused by excessive work on his poetry. He describes this feeling, in 1822, as 'a confounded lethargy of low spirits that presses on me to such a degree that at times makes me feel as if my senses had a mind to leave me' (letter to James Augustus Hessey, 16 March 1822). He talks of how he feels displaced from his community because of his poetry; at various times he records his experiences of paranoia, seeing visions, anxiety, misery, insomnia and tiredness. His acquaintances noticed that he talked to himself, was distracted, sensitive to criticism, delusional and had lost his sense of identity (at times he believed he was Lord Byron or a prizefighter). J. W. Tibble and Anne Tibble classed Clare as a 'schizophrenic' (p. 178), in *John Clare: His Life and Poetry* (1956), and later diagnosed him as a manic depressive. Jonathan Bate's 2003 biography of the poet concurs with this assessment (pp. 213–14):

> If Clare were alive today and receiving psychiatric treatment, he would probably be diagnosed as suffering from manic depression, which is technically known as bipolar disorder. Whatever the validity of such a diagnosis in strictly medical terms, judging from Clare's account of how he could write enough poems to fill a book in a week but would then dry up altogether for 'a good long while', *bipolar* and *manic* are fitting terms for his habits of writing.

CHECK THE BOOK

Bate's *John Clare: A Biography* (2003) won the 2004 Hawthornden Prize for Literature and the 2005 James Tait Black Memorial Prize for Biography.

Bate speculates on a number of additional possible causes of Clare's madness: an inherited illness, alienation from his community, malaria (caught from the mosquito-infested fens), a poor diet, post-traumatic stress disorder caused by witnessing someone falling fatally from a cart, seasonal affective disorder, alcohol abuse and the possibility that he had syphilis (pp. 409–11). He concludes that Clare's madness is likely to have had more than one origin. Clare describes his emotional turbulence in 'I Am' as living 'like vapours tossed / Into the nothingness of scorn and noise' (6–7); it is like a 'black and troubled sea' ('Song: "A seaboy on the giddy mast"', 14). His poignant accounts of grief are often placed in the context of losing a lover. 'Love and Memory', for example, laments that 'now thou art from me / My being is gone' (83–4).

POETIC FORM

THE SONNET

Clare wrote **sonnets** throughout his life, having been inspired by the sonnets of Charlotte Smith (1749–1806), an accomplished poet who also influenced Coleridge. Clare's most prolific period of sonnet writing was in his later life, while he was at Northborough, between 1832 and 1837. Stuart Curran suggests in *Poetic Form and British Romanticism* (1986) that the Romantic movement coincided with a revival of interest in the sonnet. Clare's sonnets exhibit a strong sense of place, and are highly descriptive (for example 'Sonnet: The Crow'). Eric Robinson, David Powell and P. M. S. Dawson observe that many of Clare's sonnets are 'organized by a list-structure' (*Northborough Sonnets*, 1995, p. xii), and that many of the sonnets concentrate on the following **themes**: 'The landscape is sometimes one of fear: fear of prying neighbours, fear of madness, of poverty and loneliness; fear of disorientation and of being irrecoverably lost' (p. xvi). Nevertheless, many of the sonnets are celebratory, especially those on the subjects of birds and animals, and Clare is particularly interested in capturing a moment in this verse form.

Clare's mature sonnets focus on description rather than commentary or interpretation. 'The Foddering Boy' is a good example of this. Here Clare presents a scene which is completely unified, where the eye moves from the boy to the landscape in an uninterrupted flow. William Howard comments that Clare created sonnets that capture a snapshot of an 'evocative scene', but at the same time are 'transient' moments (*John Clare*, 1981, p. 121). Movement and stillness can be found in his perception of landscape. At a formal level, Clare shows clear awareness of the octave and the sestet, a feature of the Petrarchan sonnet, though he does not follow conventional rhyme schemes. The Romantic and Victorian eras were great periods of formal experimentation in poetry, and so it is fitting that Clare, a transitional figure between these eras, does this. Clare read the sonnets of Shakespeare, which were some of his favourites, and those of Milton and Spenser. Clare preferred to write sonnets in **rhyming couplets**, thus, to some extent, echoing the Spenserian form (*ababbcbccdcdee*). It is likely, though, that Clare's main influence was the **ballad**.

CHECK THE POEM

Keats's sonnet 'If by dull rhymes our English must be chained' (1819) explores the nature of the sonnet form. Keats experimented with the **Shakespearean** and the **Petrarchan sonnet**.

CONTEXT

The Petrarchan sonnet divides into an **octave** and a **sestet**, with a **volta** at the end of the octave. It was invented by Petrarch in thirteenth-century Italy and came to Britain in the sixteenth century. In English, the **metre** is usually **iambic pentameter**. The octave often proposes an issue or describes an experience, and the sestet concludes the issue or comments on the experience. The octave rhymes *abbaabba* and the sestet usually rhymes *cdecde*, though variations are permitted.

THE DRAMATIC MONOLOGUE

Closely associated with the **soliloquy** in drama, the **dramatic monologue** is a conversational **genre** that began to take form in the Romantic period, through poems such as Coleridge's 'Frost at Midnight' (1798) and 'This Lime-Tree Bower My Prison' (1797) and Wordsworth's 'Lines Composed a Few Miles above Tintern Abbey' (1798), but came to full fruition during the Victorian period. These early examples of the genre are sometimes known as **conversation poems**. Alfred Lord Tennyson (1809–92) and Robert Browning (1812–89), both Victorian poets, are the masters of this genre. Tennyson's 'Ulysses' (composed in 1833, and published in 1842) and Browning's 'My Last Duchess' (1842) and 'Porphyria's Lover' (1836) are the classic examples. The dramatic monologue is an intimate speech that provides its own context through implication; the reader must infer the nature of the location and the action. When in 'The Nightingale's Nest' the poet says: 'Hark! there she is, as usual, let's be hush' (42), we infer that the bird is in our presence.

Dramatic monologues have silent listeners (who may or may not be the reader), but, in the case of Browning's poetry, occasionally it is implied that the listener has replied in some way. 'The Lament of Swordy Well' is a dramatic monologue spoken in the voice of the piece of land. The conversational **tone** of the dramatic monologue makes the poem vivid, and makes it seem to be in real time. So, the speaker of 'The Nightingale's Nest' can part the bushes in front of us and tell us to be quiet in order to give us a more real experience. 'The Eternity of Nature' draws on the conversation poem for its inspiration. The term, invented by Coleridge in the subtitle to his poem 'The Nightingale' (1798), describes a relaxed poem which has a conversational tone. Coleridge's conversation poems 'The Eolian Harp' (1795), 'This Lime-Tree Bower My Prison' and 'Frost at Midnight' are in **blank verse**, but Clare prefers **heroic couplets**. The heroic couplet was one of the most popular verse forms of the eighteenth century, possibly due to the success of Alexander Pope, who perfected the form.

CHECK THE NET

You can read many of the poems mentioned in these Notes online at www.online-literature.com

CONTEXT

An aeolian harp is a stringed instrument which produces musical sounds when exposed to the wind. It takes its name from Aeolus, the Greek god of winds. Coleridge asks in 'The Eolian Harp' (composed in 1795): 'what if all of animated nature / Be but organic harps diversely framed, / That tremble into thought, as o'er them sweeps / Plastic and vast, one intellectual breeze, / At once the Soul of each, and God of All?' (44–8).

ELEGIES AND EPITAPHS

William Howard comments in *John Clare* (1981) that the use of the third-person speaker and the past tense in 'The Peasant Poet' 'gives the poem the air of an epitaph' (p. 150). Howard is suggesting that the poem has a sombre tone that makes it appear to be like the kind of writing that might be seen on a headstone in a graveyard. Graveyard poetry usually describes the deceased, reflecting on his or her life and loves, as this poem does. Wordsworth writes, in his 'Essay on Epitaphs' (1810), that the **epitaph** writer expresses 'truth hallowed by love – the joint offspring of the worth of the dead and the affections of the living'. While it is not known whether Clare knew this essay, it is significant that there is a strong element of **melancholy** elegiac poetry in the Romantic period, and in his work. Some of this was influenced by Thomas Gray (1716–71), whose 'Elegy Written in a Country Churchyard' (1751) is a central text of the group of eighteenth-century poets who came to be known as the graveyard poets. 'The Peasant Poet' is a good example of a poem that is influenced by this genre. The use of the past tense – 'He loved the brook's soft sound' (1) – gives the poem the tone of an epitaph.

CHECK THE BOOK

To read more about **elegies**, graveyard poets and many of the other terms and literary schools mentioned in these Notes, see J. A. Cuddon's *The Penguin Dictionary of Literary Terms and Literary Theory* (revised by C. E. Preston, fourth edition, 1999) – a helpful and accessible guide.

LANGUAGE AND STYLE

Clare's poetry fosters an intimacy with the reader through his conversational tone and the use of the dramatic monologue. As Janet M. Todd has observed in her 1973 work *In Adam's Garden: A Study of John Clare's Pre-Asylum Poetry* (p. 47):

> Usually the narrator is the perceiver in the poem, and in most he leads the reader as a friend, physically accompanying him through the scenes he chooses, toward the narrator's own perception and resultant philosophy.

Using this **trope** of implied friendship, the poet is able to condition the listener to be more receptive to his views when he explains that people have a negative impact on the natural world, and when he reveals its great secrets.

Clare's naturalness is also seen in his language. Elizabeth Helsinger writes in 'Clare and the Place of the Peasant Poet' (in *Critical Inquiry*, 13:3, 1987) that Clare's lack of punctuation (before his

CHECK THE BOOK

If you wish to find out more about the lives and work of many of the writers mentioned in these Notes, *The Oxford Companion to English Literature*, edited by Margaret Drabble (revised sixth edition, 2006), is a good place to begin.

work was edited) mimics the 'unenclosed landscapes' that his work celebrates (p. 516). We can read this lack of punctuation as a lack of education, or as a deliberate choice not to be mastered by boundaries. Helsinger also points out that the loose punctuation is similar to speech. Steeped in oral traditions, Clare lived among people who recited **ballads** and told stories, and he read his own poems aloud to his family, something which is likely to lead to the promotion of a conversational **tone**.

Personification is a feature of Clare's style, and has been a feature of poetry since the classical period and is an important element in eighteenth-century poetry. Clare personifies seasons and months ('Winter' and 'December' in *The Shepherd's Calendar*), poetry ('Poesy' in 'Emmonsales Heath'), solitude ('The Nightingale's Nest'), labour ('Sonnet: "The maiden ran away"'), emotions (joy in 'Emmonsales Heath' and 'First Love's Recollections'), flowers ('woodbine' in 'The Summer Shower'), nature ('The Parish', 'The Wren', 'Song: "The morning mist is changing blue"'), **melancholy** ('St Martin's Eve'), thought ('The Nightingale's Nest'), memory ('First Love's Recollections'), furniture (the table in 'The Parish', and the chair in 'The Flitting'). The poems also have **anthropomorphic** aspects.

Occasionally, Clare uses an elevated form of address of the type often seen in the **ode**. This is also a feature of Wordsworth's work; as with Wordsworth, these are Clare's signal moments when he worships nature in his poetry. Wordsworth opens *The Prelude* (published in 1850) with an invocation of nature as a breeze: 'O there is blessing in this gentle breeze' (1). This shares the kind of appreciation of nature seen in 'Emmonsales Heath': 'O there are spots amid thy bowers / Which nature loves to find' (57–8).

By contrast, Clare is also a poet of **dialect**. His use of unpolished local words such as 'progged' and 'clack' enables him to preserve a language that was important for the expression of his inner voice. Wordsworth, while arguing in favour of returning poetry to the simplicity of rural speech, was explicit that this should include words that were accessible for everyone. Wordsworth is, in this sense, a national poet, while Clare is a local one.

PART FOUR

CRITICAL PERSPECTIVES

READING CRITICALLY

This section provides a range of critical viewpoints and perspectives on the poetry of John Clare and gives a broad overview of key debates, interpretations and theories proposed since the poems were published. It is important to bear in mind the variety of interpretations and responses the poems have produced, many of them shaped by the critics' own backgrounds and historical contexts.

No single view of the poems should be seen as dominant – it is important that you arrive at your own judgements by questioning the perspectives described, and by developing your own critical insights. Objective analysis is a skill achieved through coupling close reading with an informed understanding of the key ideas, related texts and background information relevant to the poems. These elements are all crucial in enabling you to assess the interpretations of other readers, and even to view works of criticism as texts in themselves. The ability to read critically will serve you well both in your study of the text, and in any critical writing, presentation or further work you undertake.

CHECK THE BOOK

Peter Barry's *Beginning Theory: An Introduction to Literary and Cultural Theory* (2002) and Jonathan Culler's *Literary Theory: A Very Short Introduction* (1997) are both worth reading.

CRITICISM: EARLY AND LATE

Clare did not attract the major reviewers of the age, and many of his reviewers merely repeated parts of his editor's introductions, but it is possible to gain some sense from the period of how his poetry was regarded. There is very little criticism of Clare's writing, early or late, that does not in some sense situate his work within the context of his life.

Early criticism tended to be evaluative, judging the quality of the poems according to contemporary tastes. Much modern criticism has focused on the marketing strategy operated by John Taylor in promoting Clare as a 'Northamptonshire peasant'. Sarah Zimmerman, for example, in 'Accounting for Clare' (in *College*

CONTEXT

Marxist criticism derives from the work of the nineteenth-century German political philosopher Karl Marx (1818–83). Marxist critics focus on the conflicts between classes. According to Marxist theory, society is constructed as a kind of pyramid: the social and economic elements are at the base, the cultural aspects at the top; culture is always informed by the social forces that support it, so literature, then, is never separate from politics and economics. Marxist criticism explores what determines or informs art.

CHECK THE NET

An online facsimile of John Clare's 1820 *Poems Descriptive of Rural Life and Scenery* (second edition) can be found at **http://books. google.com** – search for the title and author.

English, 62:3, 2000), comments on how limiting this is for criticism: 'Clare has often had his works read as the poetic articulations of his distressed circumstances, rather than as the carefully crafted products of his extensive reading and sustained poetic experimentation' (p. 318). Clare is often positioned culturally as someone who fought against his publishers to find a voice for himself that was uncensored, and criticism from a Marxist standpoint has emphasised the class conflict implied by the editing of Clare into Standard English.

One of the central arguments among students of Clare's work concerns the issue of whether the manuscripts are more important than the versions that Clare published. Roger Sales sums this up in *John Clare: A Literary Life* (2002):

> One of the legacies of Romanticism is a model of literary lives in which solitary, and often alienated, geniuses labour to create works that are uniquely and distinctively their own. These works then become contaminated when they come into contact with the literary marketplace, which is seen as existing in a separate sphere. This is the view that seems to underpin the recent Clarendon editions of Clare: the authentic text is always the author's text before it reaches the marketplace. (pp. 69–70)

The manuscripts may be seen as Clare's own unmediated voice; they give us access to his intentions. The issue of editorial collaboration, publication processes and the exploration of the relationships between the manuscript and text are of equal interest, however. There is more on this below, along with an examination of the critical reception (where appropriate, both early and late) of Clare's major publications.

POEMS DESCRIPTIVE OF RURAL LIFE AND SCENERY (1820)

John Taylor wrote a careful introduction to the first volume that Clare published, aiming to manage the climate into which the poems were released. He provided a short biography of the poet, argued for the poems' 'intrinsic merit', and made it clear that they should be read on their own terms as 'the genuine productions of a young Peasant'. The *New Times* reviewed the volume favourably, suggesting that Clare was an unspoiled genius: 'The efforts of the uncultivated mind – the outpourings of genius unmoulded by scholastic system and unimbued with scholastic lore must ever be interesting to the lover of literature, and the observer of human nature' (*John Clare: The Critical Heritage*, edited by Mark Storey, 1973, p. 54).

The anonymous *New Times* reviewer expressed sympathy for Clare's 'moments snatched from the labour by which he earned a scanty subsistence, with no other writing apparatus than his hat, a scrap of paper, and a pencil' (p. 55). The *New Monthly Magazine* praised the descriptive quality of his verse, suggesting that Clare had perhaps overdone the detail: 'in his minuteness of detail he seems at a loss where to stop' (p. 68). The reviewer noted Clare's debts to Robert Burns, and commented on the use of **dialect**: 'But surely, such expressions as "bangs," "chaps," (for "young fellows,") "eggs on," "fex," (a petty oath,) "flops," "snifting and snufting," &c., are mere vulgarisms, and may as well be excluded from the poetical lexicon, as they have long since been banished from the dictionary of polite conversation' (p. 71). We can see Clare's work entering into an environment that had explicit rules on taste. A review in the *British Critic*, in June 1821, dismissed the trend for peasant verse, observing that 'Nothing is more easy than for any person, of moderate talents, be his situation in life what it may, who can read and write, and is in possession of Thomson's *Seasons* and [James] Beattie's *Minstrel*, and one or two other poems of that class, to cultivate a talent for making verses' (p. 118).

THE VILLAGE MINSTREL AND OTHER POEMS (1821)

The critics of Clare's time praised his genuine approach in this volume, and cautioned the poet that he should not contaminate his verse with **allusions** to or imitations of other poetry. They regarded his verse as superior to that of Robert Bloomfield, and observed that his poetry had developed and that he had 'read a good deal, and studied both our ancient and modern bards' (*John Clare: The Critical Heritage*, edited by Mark Storey, 1973, p. 145). One critic thought that Clare was being pressurised to produce too much verse too soon, and wished that some of the poetry had been left to gestate for longer.

CHECK THE BOOK
All these reviews are reprinted in *John Clare: The Critical Heritage*, edited by Mark Storey (1973).

CHECK THE NET
For an online facsimile of James Beattie's *The Minstrel*, go to **http://books. google.com** and search for the author and title.

THE VILLAGE MINSTREL AND OTHER POEMS (1821) continued

CONTEXT

James Beattie
(1735–1803) was a
poet and moral
philosopher.
The Minstrel, his
popular poem, was
published in 1771
(Book I) and 1774
(Book II), and, like
Clare's poem 'The
Village Minstrel',
is written in
**Spenserian
stanzas**, and
'narrated the
poetic growth of
a rural "primitive"
in a manner that
bore considerable
resemblance to
Clare's work'
(Jonathan Bate,
*John Clare: A
Biography*, 2003,
p. 220). Beattie,
like Clare, suffered
from depression.

In general, critics read the poetry biographically. Of the main poem in the collection, 'The Village Minstrel', one critic observed: 'Clare is himself the hero of his poem, and paints, with glowing vigour, the misery in which he then was, and his anxiety for his future fate' (p. 146). The **sonnets** of the volume were praised in the *Monthly Magazine*, which thought that he had excelled here 'more than in any other species of composition that he has attempted' (p. 155). The reviews, in general, show that Clare was beginning to be accepted as a poet. For Jonathan Bate, *The Village Minstrel* reveals Clare to be a 'far more versatile and accomplished writer than had been apparent from his first book' (*John Clare: A Biography*, 2003, p. 224).

THE SHEPHERD'S CALENDAR, WITH VILLAGE STORIES AND OTHER POEMS (1827)

In response to this work, the *Literary Chronicle* praised Clare for his 'native and undefiled genius' (*John Clare: The Critical Heritage*, edited by Mark Storey, 1973, p. 208). The volume was not widely reviewed, however, and by mid 1829 it had sold only four hundred and twenty-five of the thousand copies. Clare tried to sell some of the books to the people in his own village, but did not meet with much success. The book was, nevertheless, important. William Hone, a major antiquarian of the period, included passages from the work in his *Year Book* (1831–2). The poems did not, however, sustain a reputation through the Victorian period, and it was their republication in 1964 that brought them to light again. Eric Robinson, David Powell and P. M. S. Dawson call this work 'probably the most widely read and best loved of Clare's poetic sequences in the twentieth century' and suggest that parts of it, including 'December', have 'probably never been surpassed in English poetry descriptive of nature' (*Poems of the Middle Period*, Vol. I, p. xviii). This was the poem that reintroduced Clare to the reading public in 1964, when the manuscript version was edited by Eric Robinson and Geoffrey Summerfield.

John Barrell in *The Idea of Landscape and the Sense of Place 1730–1840: An Approach to the Poetry of John Clare* (1972) argues that the poem is indicative of a sense of place. By this he means that Clare's observations are particularly local to his region, and, in some cases, to his village. This was unusual before Clare. For Clare, Barrell asserts, 'a place is a good deal more than a landscape', and 'it is the topography of a place that fixes its identity for him' (p. 172). Barrell uses *The Shepherd's Calendar* to defend Clare's poetry against the criticism that it has 'no human content – the people we meet in Clare's poems have no character, no reality' (p. 172). He concedes that the interior life of the villagers that we meet in the poem is not available to any great extent, and that 'Clare certainly makes no attempt to present ploughmen or threshers or shepherds as individuals, with strongly marked character-traits of their own' (p. 172). Barrell's defence of Clare is that because the feudal system was largely still in place, people were associated more with what they did as an occupation, rather than with individual characteristics. Shepherds, for example, are depicted as lonely because their livelihood requires them to be. Even though Romanticism encouraged the interest in individuality in literature (and Barrell references George Crabbe, whose poem *The Village*, 1783, was an important early example of the interest in the individual in a rural context, and Wordsworth's poetry), this is not relevant for the society that Clare describes.

Mark Storey comments that *The Shepherd's Calendar* 'is Clare's first mature poem' (*The Poetry of John Clare: A Critical Introduction*, 1974, p. 69). Much of Storey's focus is on Clare's style and the traditions that the poem emerges from. He suggests that it is 'in many ways a test case for Clare's poetry, for the range and scope of his achievement. For if his descriptive poetry is to be vindicated, it is in this work that we must seek that vindication' (p. 88). The **dialect** words are particularly important: 'Without doubt, one of the ways in which Clare recreates the landscape from the countryman's point of view is his use of the Northamptonshire dialect' (p. 94).

William Howard in *John Clare* (1981), like most critics, regards the poem as one of Clare's masterpieces, but, unlike many, he thinks it a failure. He argues against other critics who find value in the poem 'as a sociological or anthropological document', preferring to focus on the question of whether it is an 'effective poem' (p. 73). Howard's theoretical tenets are in accordance with the structuralists and formalists (see **Contemporary approaches: Formalism**). He is interested in how a poem is put together, rather than in its wider context. The poem is, for Howard, not unified; an overall structure does not emerge from the mass of detail. He criticises Storey's

> **CONTEXT**
>
> Topography is the science of accurately describing a place.

> **CONTEXT**
>
> George Crabbe (1754–1832), a poet from Aldeburgh in Suffolk, is perhaps most famous for his poem 'Peter Grimes', which formed part of *The Borough* (1810), and which was made the subject of an opera by Benjamin Britten in 1945. Crabbe was influenced by Pope's style and saw himself as a poet who reflected nature truthfully: 'By such examples taught, I paint the Cot, / As Truth will paint it, and as Bards will not' (*The Village*, 1783).

account of the structural complexity of the poem, arguing that the 'intricately wrought' **sonnets** are better examples of Clare's skill.

Jonathan Bate suggests that the poem is important for 'its intimately detailed evocation of an ancient rural way of life that is lost' (*John Clare: A Biography*, 2003, p. 310). Storey sees it more as an 'intensely physical and spiritual' response to nature (*The Poetry of John Clare: A Critical Introduction*, 1974, p. 69), as does Timothy Brownlow: '[It] is a series of precise genre pictures, given unusual immediacy and vitality by a poet who experiences natural phenomena with five alert senses' (*John Clare and Picturesque Landscape*, 1983, p. 71). Roger Sales suggests that language is important: the poem is 'a refuge not just for old customs, but also for a vocabulary that requires preservation' (*John Clare: A Literary Life*, 2002, p. 74).

In 2006 Tim Chilcott produced a parallel-text edition which places Clare's manuscript version next to the first published edition. This enables us to see easily that the alterations to Clare's language, made by John Taylor before publication, were not particularly extensive, and were mostly cuts. Chilcott observes that the text was cut by a third, and that the editing concentrated on three aspects: the **dialect** words, political radicalism and politeness. Chilcott concludes that although a large number of dialect words were cut, they were removed along with other omissions and do not seem to have been cut *because* they were dialect words. The text has many dialect words in it, and so it seems it was not the editor's intention to remove the local aspects of the poem. Some lines that attack enclosure and criticise poverty and injustice were omitted, but again these are minor. Although these political lines are not extensive, we may question whether they are powerful enough not to be thought negligible.

Chilcott also notes that references to sweating, corns and breasts were removed. These points are important because the nature of the relationship between Clare and his editor has been at the heart of the arguments concerning the poet for a long time. A central question for critics of his work is: was Clare a 'working-class victim at the mercy of bully-boy patrons and capitalist publishers' (as discussed in the introduction to *The Shepherd's Calendar*, edited by Chilcott, 2006, p. xviii)? Chilcott argues that 'the overwhelming evidence suggests that Clare's drafts were cut, not for political but

> **CONTEXT**
> The following lines from 'June' did not make it into the first edition of *The Shepherd's Calendar*: 'As proud distinction makes a wider space / Between the genteel and the vulgar race / Then must they fade as pride o'er custom showers / Its blighting mildew on her feeble flowers.'

for far more obvious literary reasons' (p. xviii). Chilcott suggests that the poems' central **theme** is 'the relationship between natural and human' cycles of time (p. xxvi). The text, he observes, 'is poised on the cusp between ... two perceptions of time: the dispassionate securities of natural time against the passionate uncertainties of human time' (p. xxvii).

THE RURAL MUSE (1835)

This volume did not sell well, in spite of the stature and praise of some of the reviewers. John Wilson, for example, received the volume with 'heartfelt pleasure' in *Blackwood's Edinburgh Magazine*. Clare's 'are not ordinary eyes' (p. 227), he observed, and he wrote 'with sincerity and simplicity' (p. 228). James Clark, in the *Druids' Monthly Magazine*, praised Clare as 'a painter of the most graphic of the beauties of nature, – his poetry is a beautiful scene laid before us of woodland, copse, field, meadow, and roadside, with the voices of birds and the humming of insects coming on the gentle breezes, and the delicate perfume of field flowers, making the air faint with its luxuriance' (p. 240).

CHECK THE BOOK

Page numbers for these reviews refer to *John Clare: The Critical Heritage*, edited by Mark Storey (1973).

Paul Chirico, writing more recently in *John Clare and the Imagination of the Reader* (2007), suggests that this volume is central to the poet's work as a whole, and sees it as concerned with 'the poet's insecurity about his access to the world of literature' (p. 169). In more detail, the volume, he argues, is 'less about the commercial world than about the difficulties of writing itself, and the complications of representation' (p. 170). For Jonathan Bate, the 'experience of reading *The Rural Muse* is akin to ... a walk with Clare through wood and field' (*John Clare: A Biography*, 2003, p. 378).

CONTEMPORARY APPROACHES

FORMALISM

Given that much of these Notes has been devoted to the close analysis of Clare's poems, it is worth delving a little into the history and theory of close reading. The relationship between the author, text and reader is often not a simple one. The issue of whether the author's opinion matters was first put on the critical agenda by two American formalist critics, W. K. Wimsatt and Monroe Beardsley.

Wimsatt and Beardsley were the exponents of a school known as New Criticism which flourished in the 1930s and 1940s. New Criticism divides critical analysis into two types: intrinsic and extrinsic. Intrinsic is anything that occurs in the text; extrinsic is anything that occurs outside of it. Wimsatt and Beardsley play down the importance of context – historical or biographical study – for interpretation, arguing that the meaning of a work largely comes from an understanding of its intrinsic qualities, such as form, coherence and the relationship of the part to the whole. *The Verbal Icon* (1954) is a collection of their most influential essays on interpretation. The most important of these are 'The Intentional Fallacy' (1946) and 'The Affective Fallacy' (1949).

 QUESTION

Should we value the emotional reaction of the reader?

'The Affective Fallacy' argues that it is wrong to interpret a text by analysing the effect it has on the reader. The reader's response, they argue, is not part of the meaning of a literary work. Another common mistake, formalists argue, is to assume that the author's intentions explain a work. 'The Intentional Fallacy' argues against the view that the author's intentions, whether gleaned from biographical research or assumed from the text, are relevant for a text.

Are Wimsatt and Beardsley right? By looking at a few key Romantic writers and texts it is possible to highlight potential problems with focusing on authorial intention. Firstly, the author may change his or her mind when writing. For example, Wordsworth changed his politics and rewrote *The Prelude* to reflect this: there are two versions of the same poem. These are, then, two texts with two sets of intentions. Secondly, there may be more than one author, and these authors may have different intentions, for example Wordsworth and Coleridge's *Lyrical Ballads*. Thirdly, the author may not have editorial control in the way that John Clare did not have editorial control over his poetry. Lastly, the author may deliberately misrepresent his or her own work for political, economic or social reasons, and have subconscious intentions. Although Wimsatt and Beardsley's views may seem a little extreme, the above examples can be seen to illustrate problems with focusing exclusively on the author in a critical approach.

Clare's first volume of poems, *Poems Descriptive of Rural Life and Scenery* (1820), contained a substantial introduction written by Clare's editor, John Taylor. This introduction determined, to a large degree, how the press received this collection, and highlighted the biographical details that Taylor deemed relevant for understanding and evaluating the poetry sympathetically. The introduction is both a statement of intention (in that it gives us an interpretation of the poems of the volume) and a statement which has intentions of its own (in that there were certain reasons for writing it).

Taylor highlights that Clare saw poverty with his own eyes, and that he gives us 'a picture of what he has constantly witnessed and felt' (*John Clare: The Critical Heritage*, edited by Mark Storey, 1973, p. 44). Clare had, he writes, 'an unhappy advantage over other poets' in that he had these difficult experiences. In this way, Taylor is inviting us to forgive any deficiencies in the poetry on the grounds that they are sincere observations. This is, he implies, good poetry because it is **realistic**, and not because it is or is not well executed. Taylor also points out that Clare's limited education meant that his 'deficiencies are the cause of many beauties' (p. 47); in other words it is because he occasionally gets his grammar wrong that his language seems so original. Clare's provincialisms are elevated by Taylor to the status of 'the unwritten language of England' (p. 48). Here he appeals to the patriotism of the reader, and to the value of tradition. Clare speaks, in the 'popular voice', a language which has been forgotten by modern people. In reading Clare's poetry, we are put in touch with something that is valuable and not badly written doggerel littered with poor grammar and bad spelling (p. 48). Taylor admits to correcting some of this grammar, but stresses that he has done this sensitively, and even invites the reader to view the original manuscripts at his publishing house. Taylor's introduction was well judged and encouraged a favourable reception of Clare's first volume. But of what value is this document? Wimsatt and Beardsley believed that this kind of extrinsic (external) material was not relevant to a reader, only to a biographer or psychologist.

Cleanth Brooks, another of the American New Critical school, sums up the basic tenets of formalist reading in his essay 'The Formalist Critics' (1951). He suggests that 'The primary concern of criticism is

QUESTION

Do you think that background information and biography are important for reading poetry?

CHECK THE BOOK

You can read Brooks's 'The Formalist Critics' in *The Norton Anthology of Theory and Criticism*, edited by Vincent B. Leitch (2001).

with the problem of unity': that the form and content of a poem should be unified. This is because the poem's meaning is derived from its form. Brooks observes that 'the formalist critic is concerned primarily with the work itself' and not with the author's life. He argues that exploring the author's life is simply not literary criticism. The critic must, then, assume that everything that is needed for reading has made it into the text. If a poem is successful, then we must know this from the poem alone and not from any extrinsic information.

POST-COLONIAL THEORY

In his book *Decolonising the Mind: The Politics of Language in African Literature* (1986), the Kenyan academic and son of a peasant farmer Ngũgĩ wa Thiong'o said farewell to the English language, deciding to write instead in the two African languages he grew up with. He rejected writing in English because he recognised the power of this language within his own cultural context: it represented the might of a colonial power. To have to write like an Englishman was, to him, to accept that his mind had been colonised. Ngũgĩ's protest has some resonance for John Clare, in that Clare's English is inflected by a regional rather than a national voice.

The editing of Clare's writing in such a way as to make it more widely accessible has been seen by some as a mental colonisation of a similar kind. The change in language represents a change in culture. As Ngũgĩ wa Thiong'o puts it: 'Language carries culture, and culture carries, particularly through orature [orally transmitted texts] and literature, the entire body of values by which we come to perceive ourselves and our place in the world' (p. 2538). We see something of Clare's rejection of the cultural impositions on his class in 'The Parish'. Ngũgĩ describes, in his book, his own culture's resistance through native stories that he and his friends enjoyed hearing about and retelling. Stories where weak animals won victories over strong ones and stories that forced animals to cooperate in order to overcome adversity reflected the struggles for independence that were going on in his own country. Of the human stories, his community favoured 'courage, kindness, mercy, hatred of evil, concern for others', and 'co-operation as the ultimate good in a community was a constant theme' (p. 2536).

CHECK THE BOOK

You can read an extract from *Decolonising the Mind: The Politics of Language* by Ngũgĩ wa Thiong'o in the second volume of *The Norton Anthology* of *English Literature*, edited by Stephen Greenblatt and M. H. Abrams (revised eighth edition, 2006, pp. 2535–9).

QUESTION

Is the suppression of Clare's native **dialect** in some sense a colonisation of the mind? Or is it more appropriate to look at it in Marxist terms as a necessary economic manoeuvre?

ECO-CRITICISM

Eco-criticism is a recent critical school that concerns itself with exploring the relationship between human culture (and, in particular, literature) and the environment. Eco-critics admire the work of writers who try to reclaim a lost unity with nature or to find consolation in nature. They are interested in writers who record the natural world without imposing a cultural stamp upon it. Their school is, in part, a response to the Marxist–New Historicist view that nature is a cultural or linguistic concept. They argue that this view devalues the natural world and shows disrespect for it. Jonathan Bate's *Romantic Ecology: Wordsworth and the Environmental Tradition* (1991) is an example of criticism that aims to reinterpret nature poetry.

Bate takes issue with critics who interpret the interest in nature in Wordsworth's later work as conservatism, arguing that love for nature and an overt avoidance of engagement with radical politics does not necessarily denote conservatism. Bate suggests that Wordsworth's radicalism lies in his 'green' thinking: he places value on nature above all else. The Romantics construct nature, Bate says, as a paradise in which mankind is in harmony with the environment: 'To go back to nature is not to retreat from politics but to take politics into a new domain, the relationship between Love of Nature and Love of Mankind and, conversely, between the Rights of Man and the Rights of Nature' (p. 33).

Clare is also discussed in these Notes as a poet who illustrates the point that poetry 'is not only a means of verbal expression, it is also a means of emotional communication between man and the natural world' (Bate, *Romantic Ecology*, 1991, p. 17). For Clare and Wordsworth, pastoral poetry expresses the life and beauty of nature in an 'evergreen language' (p. 18). Poets traditionally explore nature in the pastoral mode, and this mode has been understood by Marxist–New Historicists as hiding politics: the pastoral is seen as 'a comforting aristocratic fantasy that covers up the real conditions of oppression' (p. 18). Clare, like Wordsworth, recognises the 'refuse of nature', the weeds, the untidiness, the ordinariness; Clare's deep respect for the natural world, which is now under threat in ways he could not even imagine, is admired by eco-critics. Romantic nature poetry is, according to Bate, not a retreat from politics but the beginning of eco-politics.

CONTEXT

This quotation from Bate's 1991 work **alludes** to Thomas Paine's *The Rights of Man* (1791–2). Paine was a British political theorist who emigrated to America in mid life; his work was influential on the American War of Independence. He argued that democracy was essential for good government and that men were entitled to equal rights. His work was banned in England and he was forced to flee on the grounds that it was considered seditious; in his absence he was sentenced to death.

PART FIVE

BACKGROUND

JOHN CLARE'S LIFE AND WORKS

CONTEXT

Ann Clare gave birth to twins in the heatwave of 1793, but it was the weaker one – John – who survived. His twin sister, who was to have been christened Elizabeth, died a few weeks later.

John Clare was born, on 13 July 1793, to a working-class family in the village of Helpston, then in Northamptonshire. His father, Parker Clare, was a thresher who could read, though was not widely read; but his mother, Ann Stimson, did not know the alphabet and was suspicious of reading. Parker entertained his son with **ballads** and folk tales, and fostered in John a love of storytelling. John received a rudimentary education, and then went on to employment in a variety of agricultural labouring jobs.

John Clare's writing career began at around 1806, but his first volume of poetry was not published until 1820. *Poems Descriptive of Rural Life and Scenery. By John Clare, A Northamptonshire Peasant* sold well and went into four editions. His publisher and editor, John Taylor, anticipated that Clare would gain some success as a result of the recent fashion for discovering untaught rural poets. *Poems Descriptive* sold three thousand copies in its first year; Clare managed to afford to publish it by using the subscription method: subscribers promised to buy a copy of the book, or several, in return for having their names printed in it. Bloomfield had achieved some success in this market, as had James Hogg. Clare received a considerable amount of advice from Taylor, and from Eliza Emmerson and Admiral Lord Radstock, Clare's patrons. The patronage of the wealthy, while helpful to a struggling poet, meant that much of Clare's politically radical verse was kept away from public view. Once he had achieved some success, Clare was introduced into literary circles. Of the Romantic writers, he met the poet Samuel Taylor Coleridge (1772–1834), the essayists and critics William Hazlitt (1778–1830) and Charles Lamb (1775–1834), and Thomas De Quincey (1785–1859).

CONTEXT

Stephen Duck, Ann Yearsley, Mary Collier, Robert Burns, Janet Little, James Hogg, Robert Bloomfield and Henry Kirke White are just some of the prominent peasant poets of the eighteenth century and the Romantic period.

Clare married Martha Turner, known as Patty, in 1820, having been forced to abandon his childhood sweetheart, Mary Joyce, possibly on account of her father's disapproval. Patty and John had nine children: Anna Maria, Eliza Louisa, Frederick, John, William Parker, Sophia, Charles and two who died before they could be named.

The Village Minstrel and Other Poems (1821), Clare's second volume of poetry, did not sell as well as the first (twelve hundred and fifty copies), but these were good sales figures for the time. It took until 1827 before his third volume, *The Shepherd's Calendar, with Village Stories and Other Poems*, was published (this sold around four hundred copies), and Clare even travelled around selling copies himself. His relative lack of success during this period has been attributed to a change in literary tastes. *The Rural Muse* (1835), nevertheless, attracted good reviews (see **Criticism: early and late**), and Clare was awarded a small amount of money from the Royal Literary Fund. Most of Clare's work was not published during his lifetime.

Another important source of revenue for Clare was the annual. This was a form of publishing, originating in the 1820s, that enabled poets to receive a steady income without having to write an entire book. The annual was an attractive book that was given as a token of affection or friendship, and which contained engravings and poetry. Many poets of the period contributed to them, including Wordsworth, Coleridge, Keats, Shelley and Byron (see **Literary background: The Romantic poets**).

Clare's life ended very unhappily. Suffering from memory loss and delusions, Clare entered High Beech Asylum in Epping Forest (in north-east London) as a voluntary patient in 1837, leaving in 1841 and walking almost all the way home to Northborough. He was, shortly after, confined to the Northampton General Lunatic Asylum, where he remained until his death on 20 May 1864, aged seventy. He continued to write poetry throughout his confinement. (For more on Clare's illness and the possible causes of it, see **Themes: Melancholy, sensibility and madness**.)

> **CONTEXT**
>
> Clare published in annuals such as the *Keepsake*, the *Forget Me Not*, the *Amulet* and the *Gem*. While the editors generally paid their poets quite well, Clare often complained that his work was changed by them and that they were unreliable with payments. This gives a good idea of the kinds of market pressures on those poets, like Clare, who were compelled to write for money.

HISTORICAL BACKGROUND

Much of the literature of the Romantic period reflects the political and historical events of the time. In some texts the political message is overt. Coleridge's poem 'France: An Ode' (1798) deals with the difficulty caused by the French invasion of Switzerland for English sympathisers of the French Revolution. For others, politics is implied. For example, in his 1800 preface to *Lyrical Ballads*, Wordsworth describes how he chose for his subjects the lives of ordinary men, and, as far as possible, appropriated the language of these real men, suggesting not only that poetry can be found in the **dialect** of even the most humble peasant, but that truth lies in their simple rural **diction**. When set against the backdrop of his early radicalism, Wordsworth's cry for democracy in literature becomes political. Romantic texts are often criticised for being escapist, and Romantic poets for being concerned too much with themselves or with nature; but much of their writing engages with the controversies of the time.

The most politically turbulent period of the Romantic era was without doubt the 1790s. In England alone, the decade was troubled by the treason trials of 1794, pamphlet wars, a major war with France, disputes about revolution (both French and English), massive inflation, the dying days of slavery, the dawning of Catholic emancipation and the beginnings of a debate about women's suffrage (the right to vote), to name but a few. All of these are in some way connected with the ideals of the French Revolution: liberty, equality and fraternity. Romanticism is as much about political revolution as it is about revolution in literary form and aesthetics.

Clare was writing mainly between the 1820s and 1850s. He is, therefore, a transitional figure. Queen Victoria came to the throne in 1837, in the middle of his writing career. While the 1790s was the era of the great debates about human rights, the nineteenth century saw the gradual granting of those rights, and indeed further agitation when change took too long. Reform of the voting system began in earnest in 1832, with the Reform Act. This dramatically increased the number of people eligible to vote in elections.

CHECK THE BOOK
Jennifer Mori's *Britain in the Age of the French Revolution 1785–1820* (2000) is an excellent introduction to the subject. Mori suggests that 'the British debate on the French Revolution, waged in parliament, the press and public bodies of all descriptions shaped the minds and social cosmologies of a generation' (p. vii).

CHECK THE BOOK
George Eliot's novel *Middlemarch* (1871–2) centres on the political and social activity prior to the passing of the Reform Bill.

In 1801 the first census revealed that approximately nine million people lived in England and Wales; by 1811 the number had risen to just over ten million; a decade later, twelve million; and by 1831 there were nearly fourteen million people in Britain. The rapid growth in population was largely due to the success of the industrial revolution. Advances were made in the production of valuable commodities such as textiles; the road and canal networks were improved, facilitating the distribution of goods and accelerating the accumulation of people and wealth in the cities. Industrialisation was a gradual process which had been ongoing since the mid eighteenth century; but at the turn of the nineteenth century the age of steam took off. Alongside this great accumulation of wealth in the cities, the landowners consolidated their ownership of the countryside. Agricultural mechanisation did not begin to make a real impact until the 1850s, but the accumulation of land into the hands of fewer people and the removal of the common rights of the poor to graze their animals meant that farmers became increasingly less well off, whereas landowners became richer.

The Enclosure Acts occurred between 1750 and 1860, and are often said to have been one of the great abuses of the period, causing much hardship among the rural poor. During this time nearly seven million acres of land was fenced off. The laws also changed the grazing rights of those who had traditional entitlements to pasture animals on land owned by one person. As well as closing off large areas of open land, the Acts caused a massive reorganisation of smallholdings. This changed the way farming was practised in Britain, and forced many poor rural workers off the land and into the cities. One of the cultural consequences of the enclosure of land was the decline of local customs. This was due to a number of factors, including increased poverty and population movement. When most peasants had 'common rights' to graze animals, they had independence and status. Until the Poor Law Amendment Act in 1834, the Speenhamland system was put in place to counteract some of the effects of rural poverty following the Napoleonic Wars. The system forced the parish to top up wages according to the number of children in a family, and according to the price of bread.

 CHECK THE NET
The Victorian Web – www.victorianweb. org – has extensive information on many aspects of Victorian life, literature and culture.

 CHECK THE NET
The Literary Encyclopedia website defines the Speenhamland system of poor relief: visit www.litencyc.com and search for 'Speenhamland' in 'Topics and Events'.

LITERARY BACKGROUND

CLASSICAL AND EIGHTEENTH-CENTURY INFLUENCES

James Thomson's *The Seasons* (1726–30) was one of the important early influences on Clare, and it was through this work that Clare had access to the classics. Thomson took his inspiration from Virgil's *Georgics* (*c.*29 BC) and Hesiod's *Works and Days* (*c.*750 BC). A **georgic** is a poem that is set in the countryside; the characters are farmers who transform the natural world through their work on the land, live simple and happy lives, and work hard. It is a poem that is meant to give some agricultural instruction, but it also gives extensive descriptions of nature and philosophical reflections. By the time Clare was writing, as Janet Todd observes, the 'georgic descriptive poem was clearly past its heyday' (*In Adam's Garden: A Study of John Clare's Pre-Asylum Poetry*, 1973, p. 9). Nevertheless, Clare took much from this **genre**, especially the eighteenth-century **neoclassical** version. This tended to glorify the agricultural life without emphasising the hard work. When, in 1823, Clare was encouraged to write *The Shepherd's Calendar*, he kept Thomson's *Seasons* in mind.

CHECK THE NET

A translation of Virgil's *Georgics* and Hesiod's *Works and Days* can be found at **http://classics. mit.edu** – click on 'Browse and Comment' and select the author and work you wish to read.

Clare also took from the classical tradition Hesiod's idea of a **golden age**. This is pastoral poetry that emphasises leisure rather than work. A golden age represents an ideal, a life of ease where it is always warm. A golden age is something that has been lost; it is also a hope for the future. Traditionally a golden age does not involve the need for agriculture, as everything is provided. One of the key **tropes** of the classical pastoral is the *locus amoenus*, the lovely place, a place of seclusion from society. The pastoral is often associated with **melancholy**. Milton's poems 'L'Allegro' and 'Il Penseroso' (both 1645) explore the psychology of sadness in a pastoral context.

William Cowper (1731–1800) is often regarded by modern critics as a pre-Romantic or transitional poet – a precursor of the truly revolutionary Wordsworth in the revival of the natural style towards the end of the eighteenth century. He pioneered the conversational style later used by Wordsworth, Coleridge and Clare, and contributed much to the **ballad** revival of the mid to late eighteenth century. Cowper suffered from depression, describing in his prose memoir, *Adelphi*, the first time he felt like this in a manner that resonantes with Clare's experiences of the illness:

> I was struck … with such a dejection of spirits as none but they who have felt the same can have the least conception of. Day and night I was upon the rack, lying down in horrors and rising in despair.

Cowper began to write his epic poem, *The Task*, in 1783 (it was published two years later). Cowper's vision of the countryside is, like Clare's, an expression of class conflict: the aristocracy use the countryside to shoot game, hunt (a custom Cowper found barbaric) and entertain. He argues that if hunting were banned, these people would find that they did not enjoy the countryside. We see echoes of Cowper's views on hunting in Clare's 'The Cottager'. Like George Crabbe's *The Village* (1783), *The Task* links together a series of **vignettes** on rural life. The beginning of Book V, for example, describes a woodcutter going to work on a frosty morning; Book IV describes the lot of the frugal housewife; and Book I tells the story of 'Crazy Kate', the solitary wanderer who shares much with later portraits of deserted women seen in the work of Clare, Wordsworth, Coleridge and Southey (see **The Romantic poets**).

Cowper's conception of the role of the poet is idiosyncratic, in that he essentially wrote to relieve his own depression. Cowper's poetics is dependent on what he calls the 'mirror of the mind' (*The Task*, Book II, 291). The poet's aim is to achieve **mimesis**: to reflect the images that he sees 'till he has pencil'd off / A faithful likeness' (Book I, 292–3), and to achieve a close connection between word and feeling. He argues, as do William Hazlitt and Leigh Hunt, that the simple or 'familiar' style is the best way to convey this. This style of writing is well illustrated by Clare's 'The Nightingale's Nest', where the poem seems more like a chat than an address.

ROMANTIC INFLUENCES

Defining 'Romanticism' is frequently referred to in critical literature as a difficult task. The word 'Romantic' can designate (i) a group of writers, (ii) a concept or set of concepts, and (iii) an epoch in history during which these writers wrote. Furthermore, the term implies

CONTEXT

Cowper spent some time recuperating in a lunatic asylum, where he experienced a religious conversion, becoming an evangelical in 1764.

CONTEXT

Romanticism was in many ways a response to the turbulent period at the end of the eighteenth century and the continued disruption at the beginning of the nineteenth. Romantic writers were preoccupied by the idea of revolution: in aesthetics and in politics. The French and American revolutions heralded a new age, based on democracy. In turn, the Romantic movement is characterised by critics as a strong reaction to the past ways of writing and living.

that this set of writers is of such significance that the period in
literary history (1780–1840) belongs to them – in other words the
Romantic period.

The Romantic poets

The traditional view of Romanticism allocates this period of
literature to six male poets, collectively known as 'the big six':
Wordsworth, Coleridge, Blake, Byron, Shelley and Keats. Although
we no longer think of Romanticism as defined solely by this set of
writers, it is useful to know who they are, and that this group
divided into two generations: the first generation being Blake,
Wordsworth and Coleridge; the second generation being Byron,
Shelley and Keats. Clare fits into the second generation of Romantic
poets, in that he was born in between Percy Bysshe Shelley (1792)
and John Keats (1795), and, like them, he began his writing career in
the first decade of the nineteenth century, coming to poetic maturity
in the 1820s. He is, however, a non-canonical writer (a writer who
has only recently come to the attention of scholars) and so is not
traditionally included in 'the big six'.

William Wordsworth (1770–1850), perhaps the most celebrated of
the Romantic poets, collaborated with Samuel Taylor Coleridge
(1772–1834) to produce *Lyrical Ballads* in 1798, which has by some
commentators been regarded as the beginning of the Romantic
movement. In 1843 Wordsworth succeeded Robert Southey as
Poet Laureate. His most ambitious poem is *The Prelude*, a long
autobiographical poem in a conversational style which tells the
history of the poet's mind. This was written in two parts in 1799
and expanded to thirteen books in 1805. Wordsworth continued to
revise it for the rest of his life, and it was published in fourteen
books in 1850, after his death. Wordsworth's poetry was greatly
admired by Clare, who thought that his **sonnet** 'Composed upon
Westminster Bridge' (written in 1802) was one of the best poems he
had read, and appreciated that Wordsworth composed poetry with
close attention to nature.

Although the writers of the time had little sense of belonging to a
'Romantic movement', it is possible to identify them as belonging to
groups. The Romantics have been divided into two generations, but
there are many other ways of subdividing the authors of the period.

CONTEXT

Lord Byron
(1788–1824) was the
most notorious of
the Romantic poets.
He is famous for his
long poems *Childe
Harold's Pilgrimage*
(1812–18) and *Don
Juan* (1819–24),
which drew on his
travel experiences.
His **protagonists**
gave rise to the term
'Byronic hero'. The
Byronic hero is a
lonely wanderer
with a troubled
psyche.

**CHECK
THE BOOK**

Jane Stabler's 2002
work Burke to
*Byron, Barbauld to
Baillie, 1790–1830* is
an interesting and
up-to-date look at
the Romantic
period.

Genre is one method; but we can also look to the contemporary reviewers: the press of the period identified, usually in order to condemn, schools of poetry with which the major Romantic writers can be associated. The critic Francis Jeffrey famously attacked what he called the 'Lake School of Poets', denouncing Wordsworth, Coleridge and Robert Southey (1774–1843) as writing poetry which contained the 'anti-social principles, and the distempered sensibility of Rousseau'. This criticism was provoked by Wordsworth's preface to *Lyrical Ballads* (1800). The association with the Lakes was meant to **allude** to their geographical location, but also to their country simplicity. Southey, Wordsworth and Coleridge clearly had much in common, especially at the start of their careers; they often collaborated on their poetry. But as they progressed, they diverged to a great degree in subject matter, philosophy and aesthetics.

Another collective term in use during this period, found in a series of hostile reviews by John Gibson Lockhart in *Blackwood's Edinburgh Magazine* in 1817 and John Wilson Croker in the *Quarterly Review*, was the 'Cockney school'. This label was aimed at the essayist William Hazlitt (1778–1830), the poet and essayist Leigh Hunt (1784–1859), and the poet John Keats (1795–1821). It refers to their humble origins, supposedly 'vulgar' **diction**, 'loose … versification' and cockney rhymes. Lockhart dismisses Keats as 'the meanest, the filthiest, and one of the most vulgar of Cockney poetasters'. Keats, who was largely self-taught, had not had the traditional classical education required for a man of letters, and is criticised for attempting to write in the classical vein.

A further group of poets was termed the 'Satanic school' and included Lord George Gordon Byron (1788–1824) and Percy Bysshe Shelley (1792–1822) and their followers. The group arose as part of the dispute between Southey and Byron. Southey's preface to *A Vision of Judgement* (1821), his **eulogy** on the death of George III, written when he was Poet Laureate and a staunch member of the Establishment, is a thinly veiled attack on Byron, whom he saw as satanic because of his libertine lifestyle and morally daring poetry. Southey laments that the reviewers of the day criticise poetry for experimentation in verse form (a criticism which he often suffered from himself), when they should really be attacking the writing of the Satanic school.

> **CONTEXT**
>
> Jean-Jacques Rousseau (1712–78) was an important Genevan philosopher, composer and playwright. He believed that society and civilisation had corrupted the natural goodness of mankind (*A Discourse on the Sciences and the Arts*, 1750).

 CHECK THE BOOK

Rousseau's *The Social Contract* (1762) explores the ways in which equality can be brought about, and helped to inspire the philosophy of equality behind the French Revolution. He argues here that 'Man is born free, but he is everywhere in chains' (Chapter 1). Rousseau's writings also promote the value of emotional responses in informing moral responses.

CHECK THE BOOK

The 1980s and 1990s brought a profound re-examination of the concept of Romanticism, and since then many more writers have been included within its remit, including women writers and the writers of the working class, such as Clare. Anne Mellor and Richard Matlak in their anthology *British Literature: 1780–1830* (1996) argue that the word has to be dispensed with on the grounds that more inclusivity (of women writers, black writers and those who write in conservative and/or populist **genres**) has made it misleading and old-fashioned.

Like many commentators, M. H. Abrams lays great emphasis on the preface to *Lyrical Ballads* (1800) as a starting place for Romanticism: 'Gradually the stress was shifted more and more to the poet's natural genius, creative imagination, and emotional spontaneity, at the expense of the opposing attributes of judgment, learning, and artful restraints (*The Mirror and the Lamp: Romantic Theory and the Critical Tradition*, 1953, p. 21). In his preface, Wordsworth declares that 'all good poetry is the spontaneous overflow of powerful feelings'. These, he says, should be 'recollected in tranquillity'. The artist draws on his own feelings in order to create, and these feelings are in excess. Romanticism is, then, focused on the internal, the personal, the sincere: that which is expressive of the self. It is, fundamentally, **lyrical**. Clare's poetry corresponds to this definition in many ways: sincerity, a profound appreciation of nature, simplicity and deep feeling are paramount to Clare's poetics.

It is important, however, not to underestimate the pull of the external world. Wordsworth was also a public poet; in his preface he insists that 'Poets do not write for Poets alone, but for men'. Shelley similarly saw the poet as a public figure, a 'legislator', and, like Coleridge, saw the poet as the herald of a new age. Clare, likewise, was a political poet, as his writing on enclosure shows. In Romantic theory, then, personal emotion combines with a public vision to produce poetry which expresses the imagination. As Shelley writes: 'Poetry, in a general sense, may be defined to be "the expression of the Imagination"' (*A Defence of Poetry*, written in 1821 and published in 1840). The effect of the imagination, for the Romantics, is often harmony. It is no surprise, as Abrams points out, that many of the poets constructed their poetics around images of music, as Clare does. Hazlitt declares in his essay 'On Poetry in General' (an essay which served as an introduction to his *Lectures on the English Poets*, 1818) that poetry is 'the music of language', and Coleridge looks to the aeolian harp as a **symbol**, an instrument played by the wind, emphasising its naturalness, as does Shelley.

The Romantic poet must also, according to the poetics of the period, be an observer. He or she must look at nature, experience the world at first hand and record it accurately in all its detail. The inclusion of detail enables the natural world to be placed to the fore, as we see in the poetry of Clare. Reacting against eighteenth-century neoclassicism, which tended towards the general, preferring types to individuals and past excellence to future novelty, the Romantics emphasised the natural, the diverse and the real. There are many examples of this in Romantic literature. Blake's annotations to Joshua Reynolds's *Discourses on Art* and Charles Lamb's comments on Johnson's edition of Shakespeare are some of the best. The Romantic reaction both against abstraction and against the **neoclassical** 'ideal' theory can be seen more widely as Romantic individualism.

Romantic prose writers

Clare makes much in his poetry of having the freedom to wander. This was something that came naturally to him, but it is also a significant **trope** in Romantic literature. There are many examples of this. Fanny Burney's *The Wanderer* (1814) describes how a woman without a character (a good reputation), job references or male supporters finds it difficult to sustain herself, and is forced to wander when these important social factors are no longer available to her. The radical philosopher and novelist William Godwin (1756–1836) approached the same subject using a male central character in *The Adventures of Caleb Williams* (1794). This radical novel of the 1790s, inspired by the drive for equality that came out of the French Revolution and by Godwin's philosophy, explored these social structures extensively. Wandering is also associated with extreme passion in this period. Charlotte Smith's *Desmond* (1792) and Eliza Fenwick's *Secresy* (1795) both include male wanderers as case studies of emotional obsession, and Marianne Dashwood wanders at moments of heightened emotion in Jane Austen's *Sense and Sensibility* (1811). Wandering is also a feature of Mary Shelley's *Frankenstein* (1818). Shelley, who was Godwin's daughter, looks at wandering as the effect of madness, the lack of a family, extreme emotion and desperation. For Clare, wandering is to be politically free to walk without curtailment by the boundaries of ownership.

For the essayist William Hazlitt, nature is 'deep, obscure, and infinite' and should be represented as such ('On Genius and Common Sense', *Table Talk*, 1821–2). Clare explores this concept in 'The Eternity of Nature', 'The Nightingale's Nest' and

CHECK THE POEM
Wordsworth and Coleridge were also fascinated by wandering. See Wordsworth's autobiographical epic *The Prelude* (published in 1850), which follows his travels around Britain and Europe; and Coleridge's *The Rime of the Ancient Mariner* (1798), which concentrates on a wanderer character as a bearer of insight and an example of a madman.

CHECK THE BOOK

Hazlitt's view of the artist is concerned with the 'ever shifting forms of an eternal principle, that which is seen but for a moment, but dwells in the heart always, and is only seized as it passes by strong and secret sympathy' ('The Indian Jugglers' in *Table Talk*; see William Hazlitt's *Complete Works*, edited by P. P. Howe, Book VIII, 1930–4, p. 82).

'Emmonsales Heath'. In defining nature as all-inclusive, Hazlitt abandons the boundary between man and nature, stressing the complexity and variety of nature and inevitably linking this to the individuality of mankind. Hazlitt's artist 'remarks fifty things which escape common eyes' (*Complete Works*, edited by P. P. Howe, Book IV, 1930–4, p. 73). He emphasises the individual rather than the class; the extreme rather than the average. Hazlitt's belief in individualism caused him to reject all 'closed systems of thought' generally.

CLARE AS A VICTORIAN

Clare entered High Beech Asylum in Epping Forest as a voluntary patient in 1837, the year that Queen Victoria came to the throne. His isolation makes it difficult to determine the extent to which he was influenced by Victorian tastes, though he was aware of Queen Victoria's visit to Northampton when he was in the Northampton General Lunatic Asylum in 1844 (see 'Song: On the Occasion of the Queen's Visit to Northampton' and 'The Raree Show', both 1844). Jonathan Bate suggests that in the last two months of Clare's stay at High Beech (1841), Alfred Lord Tennyson (1809–92), the next Poet Laureate after Wordsworth, also stayed in the village (*John Clare: A Biography*, 2003, pp. 431–2). Tennyson suffered from depression, as did his brother Septimus, who became a patient at the asylum. It is not known whether the poets met each other. Much of Clare's later years were taken up with his obsession with Byron. He wrote imitations of Byron's work and even believed that he was Byron. Clare's admiration for Wordsworth, who did not die until 1850, was sustained in the Victorian period. He wrote, for example, a dedicatory **sonnet** which declares: 'Wordsworth I love; his books are like the fields' (1). Clare continued into the Victorian period with the **themes** and subject matter that had preoccupied him throughout his writing career.

The Victorian age was one of industry, and many of the great Victorian novels published during Clare's lifetime describe the effect of mass industrialisation on both rural and metropolitan landscapes. Mrs Gaskell's *Cranford* (1851–3) anticipates the coming of the railway to a small Cheshire town, while Charles Dickens's *Dombey and Son* (1846–8) describes in graphic detail the effect of the steam engine on the city of London (Chapters 6 and 15). Perhaps closest to Clare and his love of the countryside are the novels of Thomas Hardy and the Brontës. The Brontës' landscape is wild, stormy and passionate – but also 'local' (see the characters of Nelly Dean and Joseph in Emily Brontë's 1847 novel *Wuthering Heights*, who speak in Yorkshire **dialect**) – while in his late nineteenth-century novels Hardy echoes Clare in his deep love of the (Wessex) countryside, his appreciation of man's relationship with it, and his support for rural customs and traditions, themes also present in his poetry.

CHECK THE BOOK

See Hardy's novels *The Return of the Native* (1878) and *The Mayor of Casterbridge* (1886), and a collection of his poetry, for example the 1998 Everyman's *Selected Poems* edition, edited by Norman Page.

World events	John Clare's life	Literary events
		1791 Robert Burns's 'Tam o' Shanter' published; Thomas Paine, *The Rights of Man* (first part)
1793 Execution of Louis XVI and Marie Antoinette; Britain at war with France	**1793** Born in Helpston on 13 July	**1793** William Godwin, *Enquiry Concerning Political Justice*; William Wordsworth, *Descriptive Sketches*
1794 Suspension of Habeas Corpus Act (until 1801); treason trials		**1794** William Blake, *Songs of Innocence and of Experience*; Godwin, *The Adventures of Caleb Williams*
1795 Seditious Meetings Act and Treasonable Practices Act ('Gagging Acts'); bread riots in France		**1795** Charlotte Smith, *Rural Walks*; Robert Southey, *Poems*
		1796 Samuel Taylor Coleridge, *Poems on Various Subjects*; Paine, *Agrarian Justice*
	1797 Mary Joyce born	**1797** Coleridge, *Poems*
1798 France invades Switzerland	**1798** Starts his schooling in village dame school	**1798** Wordsworth and Coleridge publish *Lyrical Ballads*
1799 Napoleon becomes first consul in France	**1799** Martha 'Patty' Turner is born	**1799** William Cowper writes 'The Castaway' (published 1803)
	1800 Attends school in Glinton	**1800** Robert Bloomfield, *The Farmer's Boy*; Wordsworth publishes preface to *Lyrical Ballads*
1801 Act of Union between Britain and Ireland; first census reveals approximately 9 million in England and Wales		**1801** Southey, *Thalaba the Destroyer*

CHRONOLOGY

World events	John Clare's life	Literary events
1802 Peace between Britain and France		
1803 War resumes between Britain and France		
1804 Napoleon proclaimed emperor of France		
1805 Battle of Trafalgar		**1805** Wordsworth finishes complete draft of *The Prelude*
	1806 Employed as plough-boy at Woodcroft Castle	**1806** Sir Walter Scott, *Ballads and Lyrical Pieces*
1807 Abolition of slave trade in British Empire	**1807** Apprentice gardener at Burghley House	**1807** Charles and Mary Lamb, *Tales from Shakespeare*
1809 Act of Enclosure that enclosed land in Helpston area passed		
1810 George III goes permanently insane		**1810** George Crabbe, *The Borough*
1811 Luddite riots; beginning of the Regency		**1811** Jane Austen, *Sense and Sensibility*
1812 Napoleon invades Russia; United States declares war on Britain	**1812** Enlists in the Eastern Regiment of Northamptonshire Local Militia (army reserve force)	**1812** Lord Byron, *Childe Harold's Pilgrimage* (first two cantos)
		1813 Austen, *Pride and Prejudice*
1815 Battle of Waterloo; Napoleon exiled; Corn Law passed		
1816 England in recession	**1816** Relationship with Mary Joyce ends; works again as gardener at Burghley House	**1816** Austen, *Emma*; Scott, *The Antiquary*
1817 Suspension of Habeas Corpus Act (until 1818)	**1817** Works as a lime burner at Bridge Casterton; meets Patty Turner	**1817** Coleridge, *Biographia Literaria*; John Keats, *Poems*

World events	John Clare's life	Literary events
		1818 William Hazlitt, *Lectures on the English Poets*; Mary Shelley, *Frankenstein*
1819 Peterloo Massacre		
1820 Death of George III	**1820** *Poems Descriptive of Rural Life and Scenery* published; marries Patty Turner; granted annuity by Marquis of Exeter; visits London for the first time; first child, Anna Maria, born	**1820** Keats, *Lamia, Isabella, The Eve of St Agnes, and Other Poems*; Percy Bysshe Shelley, *Prometheus Unbound and Other Poems*
1821 Death of Napoleon	**1821** *The Village Minstrel and Other Poems* published; birth of a son, who does not live beyond a day	**1821** Leigh Hunt, *The Months*; Shelley, *A Defence of Poetry*
	1822 Second visit to London, where he meets Charles Lamb, William Hazlitt and Thomas Hood; birth of daughter Eliza Louisa	
1824 Vagrancy Act	**1824** Birth of son Frederick; sees Byron's funeral in London; meets Coleridge and De Quincey	**1824** James Hogg, *The Private Memoirs and Confessions of a Justified Sinner*
1825 First passenger train in Britain		**1825–6** William Hone, *The Every-Day Book*
	1826 Birth of son John	**1826** Felicia Hemans, 'Casabianca'
1827 Death of Ludwig van Beethoven	**1827** *The Shepherd's Calendar, with Village Stories and Other Poems* published; finishes 'The Parish' (unpublished during his lifetime)	

World events	John Clare's life	Literary events
	1828 Birth of son William Parker	
1829 Catholic Emancipation (Relief) Act		1829 Hogg, *The Shepherd's Calendar*
1830 Death of George IV; accession of William IV	1830 Birth of daughter Sophia; period of severe mental illness	1830 William Cobbett, *Rural Rides*
1832 Reform Act	1832 Moves to Northborough	
1833 Abolition of slavery in British Empire	1833 Birth of son Charles	
1834 Poor Law Amendment Act		
	1835 *The Rural Muse* published; birth and death of an unnamed child; awarded £50 from the Royal Literary Fund; mother dies	
1837 Accession of Queen Victoria	1837 Admitted to High Beech Asylum in Epping Forest	1837 Thomas Carlyle, *A History of the French Revolution*
1838 People's Charter issued by the Chartists	1838 Mary Joyce dies	
1840 Queen Victoria marries Prince Albert		
	1841 Escapes asylum and walks back to Northborough; taken to Northampton General Lunatic Asylum	
1842 Chartist riots		1842 Alfred Tennyson, *Poems*
	1843 Son Frederick dies	
	1844 Daughter Anna Maria dies	1844 Elizabeth Barrett Browning, *Poems*
1845–9 Potato famine in Ireland		
1846 Repeal of Corn Laws	1846 Father dies	1846–8 Charles Dickens, *Dombey and Son*

World events	John Clare's life	Literary events
		1847 Charlotte Brontë, *Jane Eyre*; Emily Brontë, *Wuthering Heights*
1848 Uprising in Ireland; revolutions on the continent		**1848** Karl Marx and Friedrich Engels, *Communist Manifesto*; Pre-Raphaelite Brotherhood founded by Dante Gabriel Rossetti, William Holman Hunt and Sir John Everett Millais
		1850 Tennyson, *In Memoriam*; Wordsworth's *The Prelude* published; Tennyson succeeds Wordsworth as Poet Laureate
1851 Great Exhibition at Crystal Palace, Hyde Park		**1851–3** Gaskell, *Cranford*
	1852 Son Charles dies	
		1853 Gaskell, *Ruth*
1854 Britain enters Crimean War		**1854** Dickens, *Hard Times*
		1855 Walt Whitman, *Leaves of Grass*
		1857 Gustave Flaubert, *Madame Bovary*
		1859 Charles Darwin, *On the Origin of Species by Means of Natural Selection*
		1860 George Eliot, *The Mill on the Floss*
1861 American Civil War begins		**1860–1** Dickens, *Great Expectations*
	1864 Clare dies on 20 May	
	1865 Frederick Martin's *Life of John Clare* published	

EDITIONS OF WORK BY JOHN CLARE

Major Works, edited by Eric Robinson and David Powell, Oxford University Press, Oxford, 1984
> Contains a wide selection of Clare's poetry and prose, including letters and autobiographical writings, and has some useful annotations

Northborough Sonnets, edited by Eric Robinson, David Powell and P. M. S. Dawson, Carcanet Press, Manchester, 1995
> Contains all the **sonnets** written by Clare between 1832 and 1837, with the exception of those included in *The Rural Muse* and *The Midsummer Cushion*

Poems of the Middle Period, edited by Eric Robinson, David Powell and P. M. S. Dawson, 5 vols., Clarendon Press, Oxford, 1996–2003
> Covers the period of Clare's life when he was arguably at his most creative; includes his poem 'Fame'

The Shepherd's Calendar, edited by Eric Robinson and Geoffrey Summerfield, Oxford University Press, Oxford, 1964
> This edition reintroduced Clare to the reading public

The Shepherd's Calendar, edited by Tim Chilcott, Carcanet Press, Manchester, 2006
> Clare's final manuscript is printed alongside the 1827 published version

Autobiographical Writings, edited by Eric Robinson, Oxford University Press, Oxford, 1983
> Gathers together all of Clare's autobiographical prose, including his *Sketches*

John Clare: By Himself, edited by Eric Robinson and David Powell, Carcanet Press, Manchester, 2002
> Brings together all of Clare's important autobiographical writing, including extracts from his asylum letters, maps of his countryside, and his will

John Clare's Birds, edited by Eric Robinson and Richard Fitter, Oxford University Press, Oxford, 1982
> Clare's keen observations produce some vivid and distinctive descriptions of birds and landscape

The Natural History Prose Writings of John Clare, edited by Margaret Grainger, Clarendon Press, Oxford, 1983
> Contains Clare's natural history letters and various writings on the natural world

The Prose of John Clare, edited by J. W. and Anne Tibble, Routledge & Kegan Paul, London, 1951

  Includes illustrations and notes

The Letters of John Clare, edited by J. W. and Anne Tibble, Routledge & Kegan Paul, London, 1970

  Originally published in 1951, this edition comprises 249 letters

The Letters of John Clare, edited by Mark Storey, Clarendon Press, Oxford, 1985

  The standard edition of Clare's letters

WIDER READING

ROMANTIC AND VICTORIAN POETRY: ANTHOLOGIES

British Literature: 1780–1830, edited by Anne K. Mellor and Richard E. Matlak, Harcourt Brace College Publishers, Fort Worth, 1996

  An anthology that revises the traditional categories of English Romanticism, and includes prose and poetry

Eighteenth-Century Poetry: An Annotated Anthology, edited by David Fairer and Christine Gerrard, Blackwell Publishing, Oxford, second edition, 2004

  Has detailed notes and a very useful themed contents, and includes writing by poets such as Alexander Pope, James Thomson, Stephen Duck and George Crabbe

The New Oxford Book of Eighteenth-Century Verse, chosen and edited by Roger Lonsdale, Oxford University Press, Oxford, 1984

  Contains poems by many of the poets mentioned in these Notes, including Jonathan Swift, William Collins, William Cowper, Anna Barbauld and Ann Yearsley

The Norton Anthology of English Literature, edited by Stephen Greenblatt and M. H. Abrams, Vol. 2, W. W. Norton & Co., New York, revised eighth edition, 2006

  Includes extracts from a wide range of Romantic poets

Romanticism: An Anthology, edited by Duncan Wu, Blackwell Publishing, Oxford, 1995, third edition, 2006

  Includes poetry by a selection of major women Romantic writers such as Charlotte Smith and Felicia Hemans, as well as prose extracts from authors such as Edmund Burke and William Hazlitt

ROMANTIC AND VICTORIAN POETRY: KEY TEXTS

There are numerous editions of collected works of the major Romantic and Victorian poets, most with valuable introductions and notes; the following titles are just a selection. For connections and comparisons with the poetry of John Clare, see the relevant pages of these Notes (provided in bold below):

William Blake, *Songs of Innocence and of Experience*, edited by Geoffrey Keynes, Oxford University Press, Oxford, 1970 **(p. 13)**
> *Songs of Innocence* (first published in 1789) lat22er became a joint collection with *Songs of Experience* in 1794

Robert Browning, *Selected Poems*, edited by W. E. Williams, Penguin Classics, London, 2000 **(p. 112)**
> Contains 'My Last Duchess' and 'Porphyria's Lover'

Lord Byron, *The Major Works*, edited by Jerome J. McGann, Oxford University Press, Oxford, 2000 **(pp. 66, 132)**
> Includes all of Byron's major poems, as well as letters and other prose

John Keats, *The Complete Poems*, edited by John Barnard, Penguin, Harmondsworth, third edition, 1988 **(pp. 23, 27, 38, 69, 77, 81, 84, 97, 108, 111)**
> Contains all poems, as well as extensive and useful notes and extracts of Keats's letters

Percy Bysshe Shelley, *The Mayor Works*, edited by Zachary Leader and Michael O'Neill, Oxford University Press, Oxford, 2003 **(pp. 11, 33, 84, 132, 134)**
> Includes *Prometheus Unbound* and *Adonais* and a wide range of Shelley's shorter poems, as well as much of his major prose, including *A Defence of Poetry*

Alfred Lord Tennyson, *Selected Poems*, edited by Aidan Day, Penguin Classics, London, 1991 **(pp. 109, 112)**
> Contains *In Memoriam* and 'Ulysses'

William Wordsworth and Samuel Taylor Coleridge, *Lyrical Ballads*, Penguin, London, 2006 **(pp. 68, 75, 82, 97, 105, 122, 132, 134)**
> Reproduces the poems in the form in which they first appeared in 1798

ROMANTIC AND VICTORIAN NON-FICTION: KEY TEXTS

Edmund Burke, *A Philosophical Enquiry into the Origin of Our Ideas of the Sublime and Beautiful*, 1857 **(pp. 77, 80)**
> Routledge has produced an authoritative edition of Burke's original treatise, published in 2008 under the abbreviated title *A Philosopical Enquiry into the Sublime and Beautiful*

William Cowper, *The Letters and Prose Writings of William Cowper*, edited by James King and Charles Ryskamp, 4 vols., Clarendon Press, Oxford, 1979–84 (**p. 131**)
> Cowper's prose memoir *Adelphi* can be found in the first volume, which covers the years 1750 to 1781

William Hazlitt, *Complete Works*, edited by P. P. Howe, 21 vols., J. M. Dent, London, 1930–4 (**pp. 80, 134, 135–6**)
> The standard edition of this master of English prose

Thomas Percy, *Reliques of Ancient English Poetry: Consisting of Old Heroic Ballads, Songs, and Other Pieces of Our Earlier Poets, Together with Some Few of Later Date*, 3 vols., J. Dodsley, London, 1765 (**pp. 73, 105**)
> This collection of **ballads**, songs and **sonnets** has since been reprinted and re-edited a number of times; see the Routledge facsimile edition published in 1996 with an introduction by Nick Groom

Joseph Strutt, *Sports and Pastimes of the People of England*, 1801 (**p. 91**)
> Reprinted a number of times since 1801, most recently in 2007

ROMANTIC AND VICTORIAN FICTION: KEY TEXTS

Jane Austen, *Emma*, 1816 (**pp. 23, 94**)

Jane Austen, *Pride and Prejudice*, 1813 (**p. 94**)

Jane Austen, *Sense and Sensibility*, 1811 (**pp. 82, 109, 135**)

Emily Brontë, *Wuthering Heights*, 1847 (**p. 137**)

Fanny Burney, *The Wanderer*, 1814 (**pp. 87, 135**)

Charles Dickens, *Dombey and Son*, 1846–8 (**p. 136**)

Charles Dickens, *Oliver Twist*, 1837–8 (**p. 7**)

George Eliot, *Middlemarch*, 1871–2 (**p. 128**)

Elizabeth Gaskell, *Cranford*, 1851 (**p. 136**)

William Godwin, *The Adventures of Caleb Williams*, 1794 (**p. 135**)

Thomas Hardy, *The Mayor of Casterbridge*, 1886 (**p. 137**)

Thomas Hardy, *The Return of the Native*, 1878 **(p. 137)**

Mary Shelley, *Frankenstein*, 1818 **(pp. 69, 70, 135)**

BIOGRAPHY

Jonathan Bate, *John Clare: A Biography*, Picador, London, 2003
    A thorough, sympathetic and very readable account of Clare's life and works

Frederick Martin, *The Life of John Clare*, Frank Cass, London, 1964
    First published in 1865, this 1964 edition has an introduction and notes by Eric Robinson and Geoffrey Summerfield

J. W. and Anne Tibble, *John Clare: His Life and Poetry*, Heinemann, London, 1956
    An updated and condensed version of their 1932 biography

CRITICISM

John Barrell, *The Idea of Landscape and the Sense of Place 1730–1840: An Approach to the Poetry of John Clare*, Cambridge University Press, Cambridge, 1972
    In this seminal work, Barrell reads Clare's poetry in the context of **loco-descriptive** verse of the later eighteenth century

Timothy Brownlow, *John Clare and Picturesque Landscape*, Clarendon Press, Oxford, 1983
    This study aims to show how Clare modified the eighteenth-century tradition of describing landscape in terms of the **picturesque**

Paul Chirico, *John Clare and the Imagination of the Reader*, Palgrave Macmillan, Basingstoke, 2007
    A broad study of a range of Clare's poetry

P. M. S. Dawson, 'The Making of Clare's *Poems Descriptive of Rural Life* (1820)', *Review of English Studies*, 56:224 (2005), pp. 276–312
    A detailed account of the subscription and publication of Clare's first collection of poems

John Goodridge and Simon Kövesi, *John Clare: New Approaches*, John Clare Society, Helpston, 2000
    Collection of twelve critical essays

FURTHER READING

Hugh Haughton, Adam Phillips and Geoffrey Summerfield (eds.), *John Clare in Context*, Cambridge University Press, Cambridge, 1994
> A wide range of essays dealing with topics ranging from the poet's attitude to trespassing, to his relationship with his critics

Elizabeth Helsinger, 'Clare and the Place of the Peasant Poet', *Critical Inquiry*, 13:3 (1987), pp. 509–31
> Helsinger explores the term 'peasant poet', suggesting that it is a contradictory one: to be a poet means to come from a higher social standing than Clare was born into. It is, however, an important political label

William Howard, *John Clare*, Twayne Publishers, Boston, 1981
> This study looks at Clare's poetry in detail, concentrating on the form and unity, and contains detailed readings of many of the poems

John Lucas, *John Clare*, Northcote House Publishers, Plymouth, 1994
> A concise and readable study

Roger Sales, *John Clare: A Literary Life*, Palgrave Macmillan, Basingstoke, 2002
> Examines Clare's work and life in the wider context of the age in which he was living

Mark Storey, *John Clare: The Critical Heritage*, Routledge, London, 1973
> Gathers together critical sources and reviews on Clare

Mark Storey, *The Poetry of John Clare: A Critical Introduction*, Macmillan, London, 1974
> Offers a clear and close analysis of Clare's poetry in the context of his life

Janet M. Todd, *In Adam's Garden: A Study of John Clare's Pre-Asylum Poetry*, University of Florida Press, Gainesville, 1973
> Todd argues that Clare's poetry is not, as Harold Bloom has asserted, dependent on Wordsworth, but is very different from the 'dominant Romantic mode of the early nineteenth century'. She argues that at the heart of Clare's verse is a Yeatsian central vision: Eden. Her aim is to bring Clare out of the shadow of Wordsworth

Alan Vardy, *John Clare, Politics and Poetry*, Palgrave Macmillan, Basingstoke, 2003
> Examines Clare's use of language, and, in particular, his use of **dialect**

Sarah M. Zimmerman, 'Accounting for Clare', *College English*, 62:3 (2000), pp. 317–34
> This article looks at Clare's position as a peasant poet in the context of the literary marketplace. Zimmerman argues that criticism has been so preoccupied by Clare's class status that it overlooks that he was a poet who was trying to sell his poems

GENERAL

M. H. Abrams, *The Mirror and the Lamp: Romantic Theory and the Critical Tradition*, Oxford University Press, New York, 1953
> A classic study of Romanticism

Peter Barry, *Beginning Theory: An Introduction to Literary and Cultural Theory*, Manchester University Press, Manchester, 2002
> A clear introduction to what can be a complex field of study

Jonathan Bate, *Romantic Ecology: Wordsworth and the Environmental Tradition*, Routledge, London, 1991
> In this influential work of eco-criticism Bate studies Wordsworth and the origins of environmentalism

Jonathan Bate, *The Song of the Earth*, Picador, London, 2000
> Another influential work of eco-criticism; it contains a chapter on Clare's poetry

Ronald Blythe, *A Writer's Day-Book*, Trent Editions, Nottingham, 2006
> Two essays from this study, 'The Poet and the Nest', which looks at the importance of nests in Clare's works, and 'Vagabondage in a Native Place: John Clare and the Gypsies', can also be found online at **www.vam.ac.uk**

E. Cobham Brewer, *Brewer's Dictionary of Phrase and Fable*, revised by John Ayto, Weidenfeld & Nicolson, London, seventeenth edition, 2007
> First published in 1870, this fascinating reference work has been revised and updated numerous times

J. A. Cuddon, *The Penguin Dictionary of Literary Terms and Literary Theory*, revised by C. E. Preston, Penguin Books, London, fourth edition, 1999
> A comprehensive and useful reference guide

Jonathan Culler, *Literary Theory: A Very Short Introduction*, Oxford University Press, Oxford, 1997
> A useful introduction to literary theory

Stuart Curran, *Poetic Form and British Romanticism*, Oxford University Press, Oxford, 1986
> Discusses the concept of **genre** within Romantic poetry

Margaret Drabble (ed.), *The Oxford Companion to English Literature*, Oxford University Press, Oxford, revised sixth edition, 2006
> A valuable general reference guide

Jacob and Wilhelm Grimm, *The Complete Fairy Tales*, Routledge edition, London, 2002
Contains every one of the two hundred and ten tales collected by the Grimms

Nick Groom, *The Making of Percy's Reliques*, Oxford University Press, Oxford, 1999
The first monograph on Thomas Percy's *Reliques*

Essaka Joshua, *The Romantics and the May Day Tradition*, Ashgate, Aldershot, 2007
A study of the place of folklore in Romantic literature, with a chapter on Clare's concept of fame

Roger J. P. Kain, John Chapman and Richard R. Oliver, *The Enclosure Maps of England and Wales 1595–1918: A Cartographic Analysis and Electronic Catalogue*, Cambridge University Press, Cambridge, 2004
A detailed history of enclosure

Michael Kramp, 'The Romantic Reconceptualization of the Gypsy: From Menace to Malleability', *Literature Compass* 3:6 (November 2006), pp. 1334–50
An explanation of the changes in the cultural understanding of gypsies in England at the beginning of the nineteenth century

Vincent B. Leitch (ed.), *The Norton Anthology of Theory and Criticism*, W. W. Norton & Co., New York, 2001
Contains essays from all the major schools of literary theory, including Wimsatt and Beardsley's 'The Intentional Fallacy' and 'The Affective Fallacy'

Iain McCalman (ed.), *An Oxford Companion to the Romantic Age: British Culture 1776–1832*, Oxford University Press, Oxford, 1999
An accessible overview of key topics that feature in Romantic literature, such as **sensibility**, and a useful guide to the history of the period

Jennifer Mori, *Britain in the Age of the French Revolution 1785–1820*, Longman, Harlow, 2000
Examines the impact of the French Revolution and Napoleon on Britain

Steve Roud, *The English Year*, Penguin, London, 2006
A study of calendar customs that describes many of the cultural events that we find in Clare's work, for example May Day

Mohammed Sharafuddin, *Islam and Romantic Orientalism: Literary Encounters with the Orient*, I. B. Tauris, London, 1994
A study of the Islamic 'Orient' and the Western stereotypes that characterise it in Romantic literature

Jacqueline Simpson and Steve Roud, *A Dictionary of English Folklore*, Oxford University Press, Oxford, 2000
> A useful reference text for local customs, with excellent bibliographical suggestions

Jane Stabler, *Burke to Byron, Barbauld to Baillie, 1790–1830*, Palgrave, Basingstoke, 2002
> An accessible and up-to-date view of the romantic period

Ngũgĩ wa Thiong'o, *Decolonising the Mind: The Politics of Language in African Literature*, Heinemann, London, 1986
> A post-colonial look at the politics of language

E. P. Thompson, *Customs in Common*, Merlin Press, London, 1981
> A valuable work which studies the customs of English working people and examines reactions to the enclosure movement

E. P. Thompson, *The Making of the English Working Class*, Gollancz, London, 1963
> Examines the history of the first working class in England in the late eighteenth and early nineteenth centuries

Raymond Williams, *The Country and the City*, Chatto & Windus, London, 1973
> Explores the ways in which the country and the city have been depicted in English literature from the Renaissance onwards

W. K. Wimsatt, *The Verbal Icon: Studies in the Meaning of Poetry*, University of Kentucky Press, Kentucky, 1954
> Essays written between 1941 and 1952 which examine critical approaches to literature; 'The Intentional Fallacy' and 'The Affective Fallacy' were written with Monroe Beardsley

LITERARY TERMS

allegory a story or situation with two different meanings, where the straightforward meaning on the surface is used to **symbolise** a deeper meaning underneath. The secondary meaning is often a spiritual or moral one whose values are represented by specific figures, characters or events in the **narrative**

alliteration the repetition of the same consonant or a sequence of vowels in a stretch of language, most often at the beginnings of words or on stressed syllables

allusion a passing reference in a work of literature to something outside the text; may include other works of literature, myth, historical facts or biographical detail

anthropomorphism the attribution of human qualities to non-human objects or abstractions; also known as prosopopoeia (see also **personification**)

ballad a simple poem or song that tells a story, often in four-line **stanzas**; ballads circulated as folk songs and broadsides (a large piece of paper used for news and for publishing ballads which was sold on the streets) as well as in elite literature. In general, the ballad tells a compelling tale in simple language, often drawing on stories from community life and history, as well as folklore and legends

blank verse unrhymed **iambic pentameter**

caesura the division of a line of verse at the centre that creates a pause

colloquial the everyday speech used by people in informal situations

conceit an extended or elaborate concept that forges an unexpected connection between two apparently dissimilar things

connotation an idea or feeling implied by words, beyond the literal meaning

conversation poem poetry written as if it is to be spoken, usually with a relaxed and relatively informal **tone** and style

couplet a pair of rhymed lines of any **metre**

dandy a person who is overly concerned with personal style as a way of defying social conformity and rigid hierarchy

dialect a way of speaking or a form of language peculiar to an individual or particular class or region; it differs from the standard language of a country

diction the choice of words or the kind of vocabulary used in a work of literature

discourse a formal written or spoken communication or debate

dramatic monologue poetry written as if it is to be spoken, which also displays a highly realised listener and situation

elegy a formal poem lamenting a death or written in sorrowful mood

enjambment the continuation of a sentence across a line of verse, without pause, so carrying the thought with it

epigraph a quotation or comment placed at the beginning of a piece of work, relevant to the **theme** or content

epitaph the kind of writing appropriate for a gravestone

eulogy formal piece of writing or speech that praises someone or something, especially someone who has just died

figurative when language is used in an non-literal way, for example a literary device such as **metaphor**

genre a literary type or style, such as epic, **tragedy**, comedy, **lyric** and **satire**

georgic pastoral poetry that celebrates agricultural work

golden age a time in the past when life was easy and at its best

Gothic in literature a style that includes horror and the supernatural, popular in the eighteenth century

heroic couplets lines of **iambic pentameter** rhymed in pairs

hexameter a line of poetry consisting of six **metrical feet** (an **iambic** hexameter is called an alexandrine)

hyperbole deliberate exaggeration, used for effect (from the Greek for 'throwing too far')

iamb the most common **metrical foot** in English verse, consisting of a weak stress followed by a strong one

iambic pentameter a line of poetry consisting of five **iambic** feet

ideology a belief system or system of ideas

idiom a word or phrase specific to the language or culture from which it comes, which has a different meaning from what is expected

imagery descriptive language which uses images to make actions, objects and characters more vivid in the reader's mind. **Metaphors** and **similes** are examples of imagery

irony incongruity between what might be expected and what actually happens; the ill-timed arrival of an event that had been hoped for; the humorous or sarcastic use of words to imply the opposite of what they normally mean

juxtaposition contrasting ideas that are placed together

loco-descriptive poetry describing a location in precise detail rather than presenting a general landscape

lyric a poem that is written from the perspective of a single speaker, often exploring the emotions and thoughts of that speaker in a personal way, and is often song-like

melancholy depression or sadness

metaphor a figure of speech in which a word or phrase is applied to an object, a character or an action which does not literally belong to it, in order to imply a resemblance and create an unusual or striking image in the reader's mind

metre the rhythmic arrangement of syllables in poetic verse

metrical foot a group of two or more syllables in which one of the syllables has the major stress. The basic unit of poetic rhythm

mimesis realism from the Greek for 'imitation'

motif a recurring idea in a work, which is used to draw the reader's attention to a particular topic or **theme**

narrative story, tale or any recital of events, and the manner in which it is told

narrator the voice telling the story or relating the sequence of events

neoclassical term used to describe eighteenth-century writing modelled on classical, especially Roman, forms and conventions. Alexander Pope (1688–1744) and Jonathan Swift (1667–1745) are two authors generally included in this category

octave the first eight lines of a **Petrarchan sonnet**, or a **stanza** of eight lines

ode a **lyric** poem that addresses a particular subject; an ode is usually characterised by its length, elaborate **stanza** structure, grandeur of style and **tone**, and serious purpose

onomatopoeia the use of words whose sounds echo the noises they describe

oxymoron a figure of speech in which words with contradictory meanings are brought together for effect to describe a **paradox**

paradox a seemingly absurd or self-contradictory statement that is or may be true

persona in literature the voice of the speaker or **narrator**, not the author's voice, presenting a point of view

personification the treatment or description of an object or an idea as human, with human attributes and feelings (see also **anthropomorphism**)

Petrarchan sonnet sonnet that has an *abbaabba cdecde* or *cdcdcd* rhyme scheme; also known as an Italian sonnet (see also **sonnet**)

picturesque a **genre** of writing about landscape that emphasises its rugged quality; in the eighteenth century there was an increasing interest in rural scenery

protagonist the principal character in a work of literature

psyche in psychoanalysis, the self. Can also refer to the human mind or spirit. In Greek mythology Psyche was the mortal with whom the god Eros fell in love

pun the use of a word in such a way as to suggest two or more meanings or different associations; most often used for comic effect

quatrain a **stanza** of four lines

realism the faithful portrayal of the 'real' world, in both physical and psychological detail, rather than an imaginary or ideal one

refrain words or lines repeated at intervals during a poem, particularly at the end of a **stanza**, often used in songs or **ballads**

retirement literature literature that celebrates the joys and quiet of the countryside

rhyming couplet two lines of poetry, usually the same length, that rhyme

satire a type of literature in which folly, evil or topical issues are held up to scorn through ridicule, **irony** or exaggeration

sensibility a refined and deep emotion seen in literature; the term became popular in the eighteenth century

sestet the last six lines of a **Petrarchan sonnet** following the **octave**

Shakespearean sonnet a sonnet that has an *abab cdcd efef gg* rhyme scheme (see also **sonnet**)

simile a figure of speech which compares two things using the words 'like' or 'as'

soliloquy a dramatic device which allows a character alone on the stage to speak directly to the audience as if thinking aloud, revealing their inner thoughts, feelings and intentions

sonnet a fourteen-line poem, usually written in **iambic pentameter**. See also **Shakespearean sonnet** and **Petrarchan sonnet**

Spenserian stanza form invented by Edmund Spenser (*c.*1552–99) for *The Faerie Queene* (1590 and 1596); it consists of eight lines of **iambic pentameters** followed by one line of **iambic hexameter** with the rhyme scheme *ababbcbcc*. The Spenserian **sonnet** has three **quatrains** and a **couplet**: *abab bcbc cdcd ee*

stanza in a poem when lines of verse are grouped together into units these units are called stanzas. They usually follow a pattern with a fixed number of lines and a set number of **metrical feet** within each line

sublime the description of nature as overpowering or awe-inspiring

symbol something that represents something else by association

symbolism investing material objects with abstract powers and meanings greater than their own; allowing a complex idea to be represented by a single object

synecdoche a figure of speech in which the part stands for the whole

syntax the arrangement of words within a sentence

tetrameter a line of four **metrical feet**

theme a subject or idea of a work, which may or may not be explicit. A text may contain several themes

tone the overall effect, usually applied to language

tragedy in its original sense, a drama dealing with elevated actions and emotions and characters of high social standing in which a terrible outcome becomes inevitable as a result of an unstoppable sequence of events and a fatal flaw in the personality of the **protagonist**. More recently, tragedy has come to include courses of events happening to ordinary individuals that are inevitable because of social and cultural conditions or natural disasters

trimeter a line containing three **metrical feet**

triplet three lines of rhyming verse

trope **figurative** or **metaphorical** language

vignette a short evocative description or composition

volta the turning point in a **sonnet** which separates the **octave** from the **sestet**

Essaka Joshua is a Professor in the English Department and the Philosophy Department at the University of Notre Dame in the USA. She has a BA and an MA from Oxford University and a PhD from the University of Birmingham, and is the author of several books and articles on Romantic and Victorian literature. These include books examining the Romantics and the May Day tradition and the history of the Pygmalion narrative in nineteenth-century English literature.

GCSE

Maya Angelou
I Know Why the Caged Bird Sings

Jane Austen
Pride and Prejudice

Alan Ayckbourn
Absent Friends

Elizabeth Barrett Browning
Selected Poems

Robert Bolt
A Man for All Seasons

Harold Brighouse
Hobson's Choice

Charlotte Brontë
Jane Eyre

Emily Brontë
Wuthering Heights

Brian Clark
Whose Life is it Anyway?

Robert Cormier
Heroes

Shelagh Delaney
A Taste of Honey

Charles Dickens
David Copperfield
Great Expectations
Hard Times
Oliver Twist
Selected Stories

Roddy Doyle
Paddy Clarke Ha Ha Ha

George Eliot
Silas Marner
The Mill on the Floss

Anne Frank
The Diary of a Young Girl

William Golding
Lord of the Flies

Oliver Goldsmith
She Stoops to Conquer

Willis Hall
The Long and the Short and the Tall

Thomas Hardy
Far from the Madding Crowd
The Mayor of Casterbridge
Tess of the d'Urbervilles
The Withered Arm and other Wessex Tales

L. P. Hartley
The Go-Between

Seamus Heaney
Selected Poems

Susan Hill
I'm the King of the Castle

Barry Hines
A Kestrel for a Knave

Louise Lawrence
Children of the Dust

Harper Lee
To Kill a Mockingbird

Laurie Lee
Cider with Rosie

Arthur Miller
The Crucible
A View from the Bridge

Robert O'Brien
Z for Zachariah

Frank O'Connor
My Oedipus Complex and Other Stories

George Orwell
Animal Farm

J.B. Priestley
An Inspector Calls
When We Are Married

Willy Russell
Educating Rita
Our Day Out

J. D. Salinger
The Catcher in the Rye

William Shakespeare
Henry IV Part I
Henry V
Julius Caesar
Macbeth
The Merchant of Venice
A Midsummer Night's Dream
Much Ado About Nothing
Romeo and Juliet
The Tempest
Twelfth Night

George Bernard Shaw
Pygmalion

Mary Shelley
Frankenstein

R. C. Sherriff
Journey's End

Rukshana Smith
Salt on the snow

John Steinbeck
Of Mice and Men

Robert Louis Stevenson
Dr Jekyll and Mr Hyde

Jonathan Swift
Gulliver's Travels

Robert Swindells
Daz 4 Zoe

Mildred D. Taylor
Roll of Thunder, Hear My Cry

Mark Twain
Huckleberry Finn

James Watson
Talking in Whispers

Edith Wharton
Ethan Frome

William Wordsworth
Selected Poems

A Choice of Poets

Mystery Stories of the Nineteenth Century including The Signalman

Nineteenth Century Short Stories

Poetry of the First World War

Six Women Poets

For the AQA Anthology:

Duffy and Armitage & Pre-1914 Poetry

Heaney and Clarke & Pre-1914 Poetry

Poems from Different Cultures

Key Stage 3

William Shakespeare
Henry V
Macbeth
Much Ado About Nothing
Richard III
The Tempest

Margaret Atwood
Cat's Eye
The Handmaid's Tale

Jane Austen
Emma
Mansfield Park
Persuasion
Pride and Prejudice
Sense and Sensibility

William Blake
Songs of Innocence and of Experience

The Brontës
Selected Poems

Charlotte Brontë
Jane Eyre
Villette

Emily Brontë
Wuthering Heights

Angela Carter
The Bloody Chamber
Nights at the Circus
Wise Children

Geoffrey Chaucer
The Franklin's Prologue and Tale
The Merchant's Prologue and Tale
The Miller's Prologue and Tale
The Pardoner's Tale
The Prologue to the Canterbury Tales
The Wife of Bath's Prologue and Tale

Caryl Churchill
Top Girls

John Clare
Selected Poems

Joseph Conrad
Heart of Darkness

Charles Dickens
Bleak House
Great Expectations
Hard Times

Emily Dickinson
Selected Poems

Carol Ann Duffy
Selected Poems
The World's Wife

George Eliot
Middlemarch
The Mill on the Floss

T. S. Eliot
Selected Poems
The Waste Land

F. Scott Fitzgerald
The Great Gatsby

John Ford
'Tis Pity She's a Whore

Michael Frayn
Spies

Charles Frazier
Cold Mountain

Brian Friel
Making History
Translations

William Golding
The Spire

Thomas Hardy
Jude the Obscure
The Mayor of Casterbridge
The Return of the Native
Selected Poems
Tess of the d'Urbervilles

Seamus Heaney
Selected Poems from 'Opened Ground'

Nathaniel Hawthorne
The Scarlet Letter

Homer
The Iliad
The Odyssey

Aldous Huxley
Brave New World

Henrik Ibsen
A Doll's House

Kazuo Ishiguro
The Remains of the Day

James Joyce
Dubliners

John Keats
Selected Poems

Philip Larkin
High Windows
The Whitsun Weddings and Selected Poems

Ian McEwan
Atonement

Christopher Marlowe
Doctor Faustus
Edward II

Arthur Miller
All My Sons
Death of a Salesman

John Milton
Paradise Lost Books I & II

Toni Morrison
Beloved

George Orwell
Nineteen Eighty-Four

Sylvia Plath
Selected Poems

William Shakespeare
Antony and Cleopatra
As You Like It
Hamlet
Henry IV Part I
King Lear
Macbeth
Measure for Measure
The Merchant of Venice
A Midsummer Night's Dream
Much Ado About Nothing
Othello
Richard II
Richard III
Romeo and Juliet
The Taming of the Shrew
The Tempest
Twelfth Night
The Winter's Tale

Mary Shelley
Frankenstein

Richard Brinsley Sheridan
The School for Scandal

Bram Stoker
Dracula

Alfred Tennyson
Selected Poems

Alice Walker
The Color Purple

John Webster
The Duchess of Malfi
The White Devil

Oscar Wilde
The Importance of Being Earnest
A Woman of No Importance

Tennessee Williams
Cat on a Hot Tin Roof
The Glass Menagerie
A Streetcar Named Desire

Jeanette Winterson
Oranges Are Not the Only Fruit

Virginia Woolf
To the Lighthouse

William Wordsworth
The Prelude and Selected Poems

W. B. Yeats
Selected Poems

Poetry of the First World War

The right of Essaka Joshua to be identified as Author of this Work has
been asserted by her in accordance with the Copyright, Designs and
Patents Act 1988

YORK PRESS
322 Old Brompton Road, London SW5 9JH

PEARSON EDUCATION LIMITED
Edinburgh Gate, Harlow,
Essex CM20 2JE, United Kingdom
Associated companies, branches and representatives throughout the world

Quotations from John Clare's poetry are from *John Clare: Selected Poems*, edited
by R. K. R. Thornton, 1997, published by Phoenix, a division of the Orion
Publishing Group

First published 2008
Second impression 2009

ISBN 978–1–4058–9617–7

Phototypeset by Pantek Arts Ltd, Maidstone, Kent

Printed in China

The author would like to thank Eleoma Joshua, Richard Cross, Tim Jones,
Sue Beardmore, Mark Storey, and the English Department of the University
of Birmingham for their help during the writing of these Notes

YORK NOTES

JOHN CLARE

SELECTED POEMS

NOTES BY ESSAKA JOSHUA

Longman

York Press